Gaga Feminism

Sex, Gender, and the End of Normal

J. Jack Halberstam

QUEER ACTION/QUEER IDEAS
A Series Edited by Michael Bronski

BEACON PRESS
BOSTON

Beacon Press
25 Beacon Street
Boston, Massachusetts 02108-2892
www.beacon.org

Beacon Press books
are published under the auspices of
the Unitarian Universalist Association of Congregations.

Printed in the United States of America

15 14 13 12   8 7 6 5 4 3 2 1

*Queer Ideas—a unique series addressing pivotal issues within
the LGBT movement*

This book is printed on acid-free paper that meets the uncoated paper
ANSI/NISO specifications for permanence as revised in 1992.

Text design and composition by Kim Arney

Lyrics from "Helplessness Blues" by Fleet Foxes reprinted courtesy
of Sub Pop Records.

Library of Congress Cataloging-in-Publication Data

Halberstam, J. Jack.
    Gaga feminism : sex, gender, and the end of normal / J. Jack Halberstam.
        p. cm. — (Queer action/queer ideas)
    Includes bibliographical references.
    ISBN 978-0-8070-1098-3 (alk. paper)
    1. Feminism—Social aspects. 2. Sex—Social aspects. 3. Lady Gaga. I. Title.
HQ1233.H323 2012
305.42—dc23   2012009320

GAGA FEMINISM

For Maca

CONTENTS

A NOTE FROM THE SERIES EDITOR

The American lesbian, gay, bisexual, transgender, and queer movement has never been only a movement about civil rights. From
its beginnings in the 1950s, groups like the Mattachine Society
and Daughters of Bilitis understood the power of popular culture. The gay liberation movement of the early 1970s understood
that the way to political power was through popular culture. It is
now a commonplace to state that queer people have always been
avid producers of culture, but the reality is that they have also
always been at the forefront of critiquing and analyzing culture.
From Oscar Wilde to Susan Sontag, Virginia Woolf to Gore Vi-
dal, LGBT people have used their "queer eye" to understand, and
explain, the complexity of how culture shapes the social, political, emotional, and psychic worlds around us. While much of this
analysis was enormously helpful in exposing underlying, often
coded, messages that were embedded in popular culture, its intent
and objective was to correct, even reform, these messages.

J. Jack Halberstam's *Gaga Feminism: Sex, Gender, and the
End of Normal* is a work that is uninterested in reform—its intent

is to be revolutionary and to reconceive of revolution now. Halberstam's love of popular culture—from SpongeBob SquarePants to Judd Apatow films to (and maybe especially) Lady Gaga—is vibrantly evident here. Halberstam is passionately interested in seeing how many manifestations of popular entertainment, which we watch, listen to, and experience every day, contain within them both a blueprint of dominant culture and its emphasis on stasis, norms, and convention, and a vivacious and joyful template for how we can transform the world into a place that no longer depends upon norms, and values maverick improvisations of difference and freedom. Drawing on anarchism, surrealism, radical feminism, queer theory, gender theory, international liberation movements, and grassroots political movements such as Occupy Wall Street, Halberstam forces us to think about how our personal investments in popular culture provide not only an understanding of our oppression, but a key to our liberation. Halberstam's background as a cultural critic, a transgender theorist, and an activist all come together here to provide us with a new way to understand the queerness of the worlds we already inhabit and the possibilities for other worlds that we would like to occupy. *Gaga Feminism: Sex, Gender, and the End of Normal* names, paradoxically, a state of living of which Halberstam approves—it is a book that brings us back to the revolutionary ideas of the gay liberation movement as it propels us forward to as yet unknown and unpredictable futures, futures that we write for ourselves as soon as we loosen our grip on the usual, the normative, and the known. Gaga feminism, with its manifestos and rants, its analyses and readings, opens up a new conversation and embraces the anarchist potential of our dynamic present.

—MICHAEL BRONSKI
Series Editor, Queer Action/Queer Ideas

Going Gaga

I've been trained to love my darkness.
                              —Lady Gaga

I am not real. I am theater.
                              —Lady Gaga

In September 2011 at the MTV Video Music Awards, Lady Gaga, in keeping with her reputation for pushing boundaries, showed up in drag as "Jo Calderone." She stayed in character the whole night, gave a long monologue about being Gaga's boyfriend, sang one of her songs, accepted awards on behalf of Lady Gaga, flirted with Britney Spears, freaked some people out, delighted others, and generally went gaga! While mainstream commentators could not decide whether the performance was cool or creepy (Sheila Marikar, ABC News),[1] entertainment blogger Perez Hilton declared that it would go down in history as one of the VMA's most memorable moments;[2] others compared Lady Gaga's performance unfavorably to Annie Lennox's drag king escapade at the Grammys in 1984. Fans, the little monsters, loved it, and generally speaking the stunt enhanced Lady Gaga's reputation as a cutting-edge performance artist and a risk taker.

The performance was indeed gutsy, especially coming, as it did, from someone whose sexuality and gender have been scrutinized since she first burst on the music scene in 2008. Who is Lady Gaga? What do her performances mean? And more importantly, what do her gender theatrics have to say to young people about identity, politics, and celebrity? Is Lady Gaga an icon for a new kind of politics, or a charlatan just living out her moment in the spotlight? This book asserts that Lady Gaga is a symbol for a new kind of feminism. Recognizing her power as a maestro of media manipulation, a sign of a new world disorder, and a loud voice for different arrangements of gender, sexuality, visibility, and desire, we can use the world of Gaga to think about what has changed and what remains the same, what sounds different and what is all too familiar, and we can go deep into the question of new femininities.

Lady Gaga is, by her own admission, a fame "monster": she is positively Warholesque in her love of attention and absolutely masterful in her use of celebrity, fashion, and gender ambiguity to craft and transmit multiple messages about new matrices of race, class, gender, and sexuality, and even about the meaning of the human. Some of these forms of being arise out of creative uses of the platform offered by celebrity; others arise out of wild relations to a series of lively objects, but ultimately being gaga means being phony.

To be clear, what I am calling "gaga" here certainly derives from Lady Gaga and has everything to do with Lady Gaga but is not limited to Lady Gaga. In other words, just as Andy Warhol was a channel for a set of new relations between culture, visibility, marketability, and queerness, so the genius of gaga allows Lady Gaga to become the vehicle for performing the very particular arrangement of bodies, genders, desires, communication, race, affect, and flow that we might now want to call gaga feminism. Gaga feminism, or the feminism (pheminism?) of the phony, the unreal, and the speculative, is simultaneously a monstrous outgrowth of the unstable concept of "woman" in feminist theory, a celebration of the joining of femininity to artifice, and a refusal of the mushy sentimentalism that has been siphoned into the category of womanhood. But this is not necessarily a brand-new feminism, and Lady Gaga herself is certainly not an architect of a new gender politics. Rather, there is some relation in her work between popular culture, feminine style, sound, and motion that hints at evolving forms of sex and gender at a moment when both are in crisis. Lady Gaga, as both a media product and a media manipulator, as a megabrand of sorts, becomes the switch point for both kinds of body futures— she represents both an erotics of the surface and an erotics of flaws and flows, and she is situated very self-consciously at the heart of new forms of consumer capitalism.

In short, my use of the term "gaga feminism" does not simply tie feminism to a person or to a set of performances, rather it uses the meteoric rise to fame of Lady Gaga to hint at emerging formulations of a gender politics for a new generation. This feminism is invested in innovative deployments of femininity and finds them to be well represented by pop performances characterized by their excess, their ecstatic embrace of loss of control, and a maverick sense of bodily identity. I can label the aesthetic categories that attach to gaga feminism as punk aesthetics, anarchic feminism, and the practice of going gaga. This punk or wild feminism hints at a future rather than prescribing one; it opens out onto possibilities rather than naming them; it gestures toward new forms of revolt rather than patenting them.

As noted, gaga feminism is not totally new, it does not emerge from nowhere (and we will encounter precursors like Yoko Ono and Grace Jones), but it certainly strives to wrap itself around performances of excess; crazy, unreadable appearances of wild genders; and social experimentation. And so, while most conventional histories of feminism are content to trace out waves of feminist thought and action that develop along the lines of social-movement histories, located in decades of action and legislation, and that emerge within or between distinct ethnic communities of women, gaga feminism charts very different territory and tracks a version of feminism that will not settle for clichéd accounts of women striking out for independence and becoming powerful in the process. No, this version of feminism looks into the shadows of history for its heroes and finds them loudly refusing the categories that have been assigned to them: these feminists are not "becoming women" in the sense of coming to consciousness, they are unbecoming women in every sense—they undo the category rather than rounding it out, they dress it up and down, take it apart like a car engine and then rebuild it so that it is louder and faster. This feminism is about improvisation, customization, and innovation. The gaga feminist, in other words, cannot settle into the house that the culture has built for her. S/he has to tear it down, reimagine the very meaning of house in form and function and only then can s/he rebuild. This pheminist takes it upon herself to "occupy gender," as the new terminology of our political moment might phrase it.

At the heart of this other tradition of feminism—a feminism rooted in destruction and refusal rather than creation and acquiescence—we find one of the twenty-first century's biggest stars: Lady Gaga. What versions of feminism does Lady Gaga package and represent? What configurations of visibility, eroticism, and femininity are arranged within her carefully managed persona? And finally, what earlier traditions of counterintuitive, anarchic feminist performance speak through and with her? This book charts what it means for feminism to go gaga, and it proposes gaga as a practice, a performance, and as part of a long tradition of feminism on the verge of a social breakdown. It also looks carefully at the new forms of intimacy, sociality, and politics that surround us but that, as yet, lack a language and so still require a figure or symbol to name and mark what they cannot speak. While I am calling that figure "gaga," it also comes in the form of "occupations" and "queer families." Gaga feminism names, in other words, a politics of gender for the postcapitalist world that we currently inhabit; it examines how new forms of family, intimacy, and belonging emerge, slowly and surely, from the wreckage of marriage, the nuclear family, and the boom/bust economy. Gaga feminism will not save us from ourselves or from Wall Street, but it might begin the work of noticing how much energy people have already put into re-imagining their worlds, re-creating their sense of a future, and reforming their expectations of how change happens and when and to whom and with what consequences. We may not yet be able to find our way out of the economic crisis into which we have crawled and we still may not be able to size up all of its dimensions, but this book reminds us that if the problem is too much acceptance and resignation then the answer must be loud and ferocious refusal. This book models the art of going gaga: a politics of free-falling, wild thinking, and imaginative reinvention best exemplified by children under the age of eight, women over the age of forty-five, and the vast armies of the marginalized, the abandoned, and the unproductive.

INTRODUCTION

One thing they never tell you about child raising is that for the rest of your life, at the drop of a hat, you are expected to know your child's name and how old he or she is.

—Erma Bombeck

Even when freshly washed and relieved of all obvious confections, children tend to be sticky.

—Fran Lebowitz

Excuse me, sir, but you're sitting on my body, which is also my face.

—SpongeBob SquarePants

I have a couple of kids in my life, my partner's children, and they were quite young when I met them—three and five years old. Both were at an age when gender is not so fixed, and so, upon meeting them for the first time, I got what was for me a very predictable question from them both: "Are you a boy or a girl?" When I did not give a definitive answer, they came up with a category that worked for them—boy/girl. They said it just like that, "boygirl," as if it were one word, and, moreover, as if it were already a well-known term and obvious at that. Since naming has been an issue my whole life (as a young person I was constantly mistaken for a boy; as an adult, my gender regularly confuses strangers), this simple resolution of my gender ambiguity within a term that stitches boy and girl together was liberating to say the least. Boygirl I am and boygirl I will remain.

Of course, as time has passed, both kids, a boy and a girl, have recognized that the world sees me a little differently than they do. When people ask if I am their "mum," they look baffled; when people call me "sir," they seem comfortable; when a teacher refers to me as "she," they roll with it but they persist in calling me "he" and their "stepdad." The little girl happily told one of her friends that she had a dad and a stepdad, at which point she gestured proudly toward me. The little friend seemed slightly confused, but then she also rolled with it: "cool," she said and turned to her mom: "That's her stepdad," she explained. The mom looked at me, I looked at her and shrugged. Life is complicated, genders are complicated, families are complicated, and yet we have so few words for these new and often quite welcome complications that accompany massive social shifts. And so we make do. We let kids who have not yet learned the appropriate languages for indeterminate identities name what escapes adult comprehension.

Children nowadays actually have a fantastically rich archive of wacky representations from which to draw as they make sense of their worlds. If SpongeBob SquarePants is anything to go by, and I believe he is, then children can find all kinds of examples of ambiguous embodiment in the materials that TV and cinema market to them. SpongeBob SquarePants and his crew of spongy life forms all experience a soft relation to reality, and while life in Bikini Bottom bears some resemblance to life above the water, it also operates according to its own set of rules, code violations, morality, and propriety. The villain of the piece is the money-grabbing Mr. Krabs, but SpongeBob and his best friend Patrick also often square off against a mean-spirited octopus named Squidward. The significance of SpongeBob SquarePants to contemporary gender norms, I believe, cannot be overstated; while earlier generations of boys and girls were raised on cartoon worlds populated by cats and mice, dogs and rabbits chasing each other across various domestic landscapes, this generation has come of age to an animated mythological universe populated by characters with eccentric and often simply weird relations to gender. And so we take SpongeBob SquarePants as our guide, following the hedonistic and cheerful sponge whose body, as he reminds one chap who sits on him, is also his face, in looking for fun, in mistrusting people who only want to make money, and in tracking down treats made with peanut butter.

SpongeBob aside, this book tries to grapple with the shifts and changes that have transformed the way we live our genders and sexualities over the last twenty years. While in universities, philosophers and queer theorists, including myself, have for years pondered the meaning of gender norms and studied the development of sexuality within matrices of normativity and perversity. We scholars don't always explicate clearly or accessibly. And that is unfortunate, because the fact is, this world within which we live, work, and love has changed dramatically since our parents raised us, and we all need a guide to the new social and emotional structures that support these changes. Just to name a few of the most obvious changes that have impacted our daily experiences of sex and gender, in the late twentieth century and early twenty-first century, we have seen a massive decline in the prevalence and dominance of monogamous marriage and a huge rise in divorce and diverse households. In the United States, we have also witnessed a new and startling visibility of transgender communities and individuals as well as new levels of acceptance for normative gays and lesbians. Gay marriage is on the horizon and the homo-hetero binary seems less definitive of sexual orientation than it did at the turn of the last century.

What has brought so many changes on and so quickly? The answer is: everything! In other words, change has occurred on account of the boom/bust economy; advances in computer technology; new medical research; increased mobility; new forms of social contact and social networking; new modes of media including Twitter feeds; new levels of media surveillance and intrusion and new forms of social control; etc., etc. Obviously, there is no need to pinpoint one singular narrative to account for the massive changes that we have experienced in our lifetimes; and in many ways, it would be weirder if our ideas of family, desire, the normal, the ordinary, the extraordinary did *not* change as everything else around us shifted, evolved, developed, and collapsed. That things change should neither surprise nor alarm us; it should *interest* us, however, and should engage us enough to spur a reconsideration of the terms, the names, the categories we use to understand our bodies, our relationships, our bonds with others, our connections to strangers, our intimacies within and beyond biological relation, and our imagination about the future. Change, indeed, is the air that children breathe, which may be why they are more flexible than adults.

But before I launch into a child-centric account of new genders, let me acknowledge that the child has all too often served as a justification for the most wretched forms of social and political conservatism in the United States since at least the mid-nineteenth century. A lesbian couple I know who live in San Francisco, just to give one example, became alarmed, after the birth of their daughter, about the amount of sexually explicit material in the shop windows in their very gay neighborhood, the Castro. Suddenly, the same environment that had made them feel excited about living in the city became the source of discomfort and concern. They quickly pulled up stakes and moved out to a suburb where the child would, according to them, be safe from the impact of openly displayed sexual materials. This is a couple that for years had engaged in a polyamorous relationship and had incorporated all kinds of sex toys into their sex life. Suddenly, however, on behalf of their infant daughter, they rushed to avoid the very materials that had nurtured their own very queer desires. We all know of the "protect the children" ruses that religious Americans have used to censor all kinds of materials that feature any kind of open discussion of sexuality— remember that in the 1970s Anita Bryant created a "Save Our Children" campaign that was designed to counteract a pro–gay rights initiative in Florida, and this was followed in 1978 by the Briggs Initiative in California, which sought to ban gays and lesbians from the classroom. Now that California has passed a resolution requiring that gay and lesbian history be taught in the schools, we can tell ourselves that we have traveled far from these paternalistic measures; and of course we have, but the problem is that the exact sex-negative attitudes that fueled antigay sentiment three decades ago now sneak new forms of sex negativity back into dynamic social systems— but this time via gays and lesbians themselves!

While we currently train teenagers to think of sex in terms of all the bad things (pregnancy, sexual diseases) that could happen to them if they actually "get lucky," many children are more wily and more canny than their parents think, and it is this genera- tion of kids—kids growing up in the age of divorce, queer par- enting, and economic collapse—who will probably recognize, name, and embrace new modes of gender and sexuality within a social environment that has changed their meaning forever.

Along these lines, let me give another illustration of the in- ventiveness of the child mind in relation to new material. My partner's son surprised me the other day. He caught me off guard. The conversation began as many others have, with him asking: "Jack, can I ask you a question?" The first time he used this approach, I was sure that some big life question would follow; or something about queerness, or sex, or something messy and unanswerable. But actually, the first few times that he used this lead-in, the question turned out to be about turtles, his favorite topic at that time (now it is octopuses; octopi?). "Jack, can I ask you a question?" such conversations typically go. "Sure, shoot." "Well, ah, hmm. How long do you think a turtle can live?" OK, so on this day, I expected another turtle question and tried to line up some turtle facts. In fact, I had been reading up so as not to be caught off guard again: turtles have been on earth for about 200 million years. Turtles cannot leave their shells. Turtles can sometimes outrun humans (helpful to know!) . . . or stick their tongues out (less helpful) . . . they can, however, climb well (who knew?). Groups of turtles are called "bales." That should cover it!

"Shoot, ask me anything you like," I said blithely. And he did: "Do you have a penis or . . ." While I tried to grapple with the first part of the question, he continued seriously, trying to come up with the female equivalent of penis . . . "or do you have, you know, a . . . well, the thing that girls have?" He scrunched up his eyes as if he had just asked a very serious and important question about planetary motion or turtle mating habits. OK. A penis question . . . "I have what girls have," I said quickly. Silence. And then: "Well, then Jack, I hate to tell you this but you are basically a girl!" True, I am basically a girl, how to respond to this while not giving up entirely on the truth of the "boygirl" moniker? Well, I didn't have to think too long. The little girl jumped in now, sensing that her older brother had reached the limits of his knowledge of such things. "Of course he has a girl thing, *he* is a girl!" Pause. "A boygirl." She said this while looking at her brother as though he had just failed a spelling test. "I know he is a girl," he answered quietly. "I am just saying, does he have a penis or . . ." I paused for a moment, wondering how to resolve this for him—the mixture of pronouns and gender categories probably needed to be sorted out. Was this the time for a quick lesson on gender, anatomy, and social meanings? Should I try to address the elephant (or turtle) in the room by raising the topics of lesbianism, transgenderism, cross-gender identification? Should I use as my example the little girl in his class who played with the boys and had recently declared girls' games to be "dumb"? I began to answer the kids' questions, thoughtfully and slowly . . . but, as it turns out, too slowly. The little guy got there first: "Jack, can all turtles swim?" he asked with great import. And just like that, the gender crisis had been raised, addressed, and dispatched and we were back to the turtles.

Children are different from adults in all kinds of meaningful ways. They inhabit different understandings of time, and experience the passing of time differently. They also seamlessly transition between topics that adults would ordinarily not connect in polite conversation (turtles and sex, for example); and often, they place the emphasis differently than adults might by making questions about sex and gender as important or as inconsequential as questions about animals, vegetables, and minerals. The training of children is as much about teaching them where to place the emphasis as it is about giving them information. But the training of children would proceed much more smoothly if there were more exchange and if adults were willing, in the process, to be retrained themselves. The whole notion of a generational exchange as a one-way process informs our ideas of parenting, and it keeps us stuck in profoundly limited and conservative models of the family and childrearing. If postmodern theory has taught us anything, it should have impressed upon us the idea that time is not linear and therefore that generational differences are more loopy and complex than we imagine when we plot them out along the straight lines of chronological age. This book advocates for more twisty, curvy, more relative notions of time, age, and difference, and it does so on behalf of an adult-child dialogue that is not

invested in a misguided and sentimental notion of childhood in-
nocence nor on account of a naive investment in the idea of truth
issuing from the mouths of babes . . . it is more a sense that
the pre-socialized, pre-disciplined, pre-restrained anarchic child
comes at the world a little differently than the post-shame, post-
guilt, post-recognition, disciplined adult. And this anarchic sense
of time and relation should be and easily could be a better model
for change than the ones with which we currently live.

While the adult filters his or her responses to sex, love,
emotions through the thick haze of training that has installed
shame and guilt as appropriate barriers to unfettered and antisocial explorations of the body, in public, private, and everywhere else, until a certain age, the child does not yet know what
the difference might be between appropriate and inappropriate, legitimate and illegitimate, important and silly. Not only
do children not know the difference, but in fact the differences
between these things register very differently for them. What the
adult considers inappropriate (eating with an open mouth, fart-
ing, touching one's genitals in public, touching other people's
genitals in public, telling someone their breath smells) may not
be inappropriate for the child. And, as Freud pointed out long
ago in his *Three Essays on the Theory of Sexuality*, the fact that
adults prohibit behavior that children want to indulge, creates a
complex matrix of desire, taboo, repression, and expression out
of which sexual personalities evolve. And as scholars like Michel
Foucault and Judith Butler have reminded us, the forbidding of
certain activities endows them with more meaning, and actually
makes them part of the child's sexual psyche rather than elimi-
nating the desires altogether.

The topics that I will take up in this short book emerge as a
series of "what if" questions, some of which have good and practical answers, some of which remain unanswerable at this time.

And so: "What if we actually let up on the training of children and allow ourselves, as adults, to be retrained instead?" If, for the child, "looks like a boy, walks like a boy, talks like a boy" equals "is a boy," then maybe this is as good a model of gender as any out there. And if, for the child, language is a playground where meaning is contingent, illusionary, motile, impermanent, and constantly shifting to keep up with the data flows that course across their inchoate consciousnesses, then maybe adults should improvise more, pick up terms, words, lexicons from children who, in many ways, live the world differently than we do, live it more closely, live it more intensely, and, sometimes, live it more critically.

"Gaga," a term newly popularized by the American singer born Stefani Germanotta, is a child word, a word that stands in for whatever the child cannot pronounce. It is also a word associated with nonsense, madness (going gaga), surrealism (Dada), the avant-garde, pop, SpongeBob; it means foolish or naive enthusiasm, going crazy, being dotty; it sounds like babbling or idle chatter. With this constellation of meanings and in its most current incarnation in the person of Lady Gaga, the term may hold some promise as a form of feminism. Gaga feminism, I will demonstrate, is a form of political expression that masquerades as naive nonsense but that actually participates in big and meaningful forms of critique. It finds inspiration in the silly and the marginal, the childish and the outlandish. Gaga feminism grapples with what cannot yet be pronounced and what still takes the form of gibberish, as we wait for new social forms to give our gaga babbling meaning. This book will explore going gaga, being gaga, Lady Gaga, gendered forms of gaga, staying gaga, and promoting gaga. It will provoke. It will be a fun, user-friendly, and quasi-academic handbook for a new feminism that offers the untrained insights of children alongside deep-seated critiques of contemporary gender and sexuality politics.

ONE

Gaga Feminism
for Beginners

Lead her away from Acting but not all the way to Finance.
Something where she can make her own hours but still feel
intellectually fulfilled and get outside sometimes. And not
have to wear high heels . . . What would that be, Lord?
Architecture? Midwifery? Golf course design? I'm asking
You, because if I knew, I'd be doing it, Youdammit.

—Tina Fey, from "The Mother's Prayer
for Its Daughter," *Bossypants*

THE *MOMMIE DEAREST* CURSE

I first floated my idea of gaga feminism at a conference at the
New School in New York City in which a host of feminists, young
and old, participated. The conference, "No Longer in Exile," consisted of huge panels and a lot of slightly random talks that failed
to add up to any kind of State of the Union event on feminism. On
one panel, Susan Faludi, the famed author of *Backlash,* spoke on
the mother-daughter dynamic, telling the audience that younger
women, by not respecting their foremothers, were undermining
feminism. She never really explained why the mother-daughter relationship presents itself as the ideal model for feminism, toxic, at
best, as it sometimes is. (Think *Mommie Dearest* . . . think Santa
Monica mom calorie-counting with her daughter and getting
her a nose job for her sweet sixteen . . . think Forever 21 moms

1

shopping alongside their preteen daughters, the daughters dress-
ing too old, the mothers too young . . . ah, yes, a wonderful
model for feminism)! And Faludi seemed to have missed several
generations of theoretical works by feminist theorists that had
moved us well and truly away from mommy-daughter debutante
politics and pushed us firmly into gender variance, gender per-
formativity, women of color feminisms, and more. Faludi also
ignored the many challenges made to generational logics within
a recent wave of queer theory on temporality. In my own work
on queer time, I have shown that queer people do not follow
the same logics of subcultural involvement as their heterosexual
counterparts: they do not "outgrow" certain forms of cultural
activity (like clubbing, punk, and so on) the way heterosexuals
are presumed to do. Rather, queer spaces tend to be multigen-
erational and do not subscribe to the notion of one generation
always giving way to the next. Other theorists, such as Elizabeth Freeman, have elaborated more mobile notions of intergenerational exchange, arguing that the old does not always have
to give way for the new, the new does not have to completely
break with the old, and that these waves of influence need not
be thought of always and only as parental.

It appeared Faludi was aware of none of these conversations,
and instead cast the mother-daughter bond as transhistorical,
transcultural, universal, blaming its corrosion for internal rifts
in the feminist project. While casting that project as a kind of
twisted Electra complex within which daughters are committed to killing off mothers, Faludi sounded more Freudian than
Freud—at least the father of the Oedipus complex, castration
anxiety, and penis envy saw these intergenerational struggles
as symbolic rather than literal! Faludi did not differentiate by
class or race; she made no mention of queer challenges to the

normativity of the family and of generational thinking; and she cast the mother-daughter relationship as some static bond between older and younger women—the category of "woman" was not in question, the fragility of family bonds barely registered, and the audience was simply asked to accept that if we could fix the mother-daughter dynamic, feminism would be alive and well.

In short, Faludi seemed out of date. And, so, at this long conference on the state of feminist theory, she floated her rather anemic idea and then sneered at the concept of a new kind of feminism, a gaga feminism that might be symbolized by the antics, the appearances, the fantasy worlds of Lady Gaga and other popular cultural figures. What on earth was gaga feminism? she wanted to know. What could it possibly offer? She proceeded to publish her misgivings about gaga feminism and her adherence to familial structures for feminism in *Harper's Magazine*. Indeed, the front page of *Harper's* October 2010 issue said it all: "American Electra: Feminism's Ritual Matricide."[1] According to Faludi's article, American feminism has a mother-daughter problem: daughters keep fighting with mothers, mothers keep being undercut by their daughters, and this, apparently, is the real reason that feminism never quite gets its revolutionary interventions right. Faludi trotted through some rather predictable and tame histories of women's social movements, surveying what have come to be known as the first, second, and third waves of feminism, better known in terms of their battles: women's suffrage and temperance movements in the first wave; equal rights and abortion rights in the second wave; and equal opportunities in the workplace and in education in the third wave. Faludi holds up as an excellent model of mother-daughter feminism Elizabeth Cady Stanton and her daughter, Harriot Stanton Blatch. After offering this vapid version of very white, very liberal feminism, Faludi then, remarkably, ends up somewhere in the vicinity of our contemporary moment, winding down to a drearily pessimistic conclusion—feminism is dead, we killed it— and punctuating this sad insight with a kind of amusing send-up of yours truly.

In her caricature of me, I am cast as "Judith 'Jack' Halberstam, a gender-studies professor from the University of Southern California who favors crew cuts and men's suits."[2] She noted, generously, that I was "the most popular speaker" at the conference, but she gives no sense of what I said and why it might appeal to the students gathered there. Instead, Faludi concluded her analysis of the mother-daughter problem with a rather predictable lament about long-winded academics who have been entrusted with a valuable archive of knowledge but who choose to squander that legacy by passing it over in favor of highfalutin jargon. She writes:

> Women's studies was originally envisioned as the repository of feminist history and memory, where accumulated knowledge would be enshrined in a safe box where future generations could go to retrieve it. That academic mother-lode is in danger of being decommissioned by the increasing disconnect between practical, political feminism and academic feminist theory, and by the rise of a poststructuralist philosophy in gender studies that prefers the deconstructing of female experience to the linkages and legacies of women's history and regards generational dynamics, and even the categories of "woman" and "man," as artifices to perform and discard.[3]

Even this critique of academics is rather old-fashioned, with its quaint notions of a big bad theoretical bully that comes along to bludgeon the good and true accounts of women's experience. Why are we going back to these kinds of quarrels, and, moreover, how did I come to be the bad guy in "feminism's ritual matricide"? As at many such events, at the New School conference, there were good talks, bad talks, indifferent talks—there was the obvious, the painfully obvious, and that was just the social science stuff . . . and so when I had my turn to speak, on one of the last panels of the day, I tried to mix it up a little by infusing the conversation with humor, a bit of provocation, commenting on what we had heard in a way that might form a bridge to the many young people who were in attendance but who seemed bored out of their skulls. While Faludi characterizes me as a glib twit who proposed Lady Gaga as the answer to what ails feminism, I actually had tried to show that Lady Gaga, in her duet with Beyoncé in the viral music video *Telephone*, provides an exciting and infectious model of sapphic sisterhood that moves beyond sentimental models of romantic friendship and into a different kind of feminism, one more in line with the intimate bonds that animate violence in films such as *Set It Off* and *Thelma and Louise*.

Gaga feminism is a politics that brings together meditations on fame and visibility with a lashing critique of the fixity of roles for males and females. It is a scavenger feminism that borrows promiscuously, steals from everywhere, and inhabits the ground of stereotype and cliché all at the same time. Gaga feminism is also a feminism made up of stutter steps and hiccups, as is clear in the world opened up in *Telephone* in both the music and the image: the off-beat, flickering, humming aesthetic that the video creates depends upon the liveliness of objects in the Gagascape (and the inertia of the human bodies), and it creates a beat for Gaga that is best represented as a sonic form of *hesitation*.

While I am not proposing that there is some kind of clear feminist program for social change in the world of Gaga, activists of all stripes and queer activists in particular have always looked to popular culture for inspiration and have refused facile distinctions between culture and reality. The Lady Gaga piece of my talk was an attempt to connect contemporary feminism to young people and students in particular by building upon the popular iconography in which many of them had already invested considerable hope. But, more than just a humorous ending to a lecture, the term "gaga" for me represented a set of wholesale changes that may be most obvious in the realm of gender norms but that also stretch to many other realms of everyday experience and that call for an improvisational feminism that keeps pace with the winds of political change.

At the conference, the students connected with the version of feminism that I linked to Lady Gaga, while old-school feminists like Susan Faludi wanted to brush this same version aside. And Faludi has not been the only feminist who is wary of the rush to find the political energy channeled by Lady Gaga. Madonna acolyte and 1990s feminist icon Camille Paglia also shrugged off Lady Gaga's appeal in a widely read op-ed in the London *Sunday Times Magazine* in 2010.[4] In her piece, Paglia asserts that Lady Gaga is simply the "diva of déjà-vu" and a copycat who latches onto a generation of glazed-eyed Internet clones and exploits its incapacity to think or know anything without an iPhone app or Twitter feed at hand. Gaga, for Paglia, represents the end of culture, the end of civilization, the end of truth, values, and meaning, the end of sex, and the triumph of a robotic age emptied of human sentiment. While some feminists, like Donna Haraway, have advocated for new forms of feminism capable of keeping up with technological innovation, Paglia argues that we have lost touch with what is real, true, and good in our mania for media manipulation, video games, and cell phones. If Haraway recognizes an interpenetration of humanity and technology in the digital age that is exciting and wondrous (even as it is also exploitative and dangerous), Paglia sees, predictably, a manufactured public realm populated by media puppets and their passive and stupid fans. If Lady Gaga's supporters have recognized in her a newish formula of femininity, phones, and desire, Camille Paglia sees only same-old, same-old or, in her words, "the exhausted end of the sexual revolution."

Why are feminists like Paglia and Faludi so wary of new figures of feminist fantasy, women like Lady Gaga or Lil' Kim or Rihanna or Nicki Minaj or Jenni Rivera or even Ke$ha, women who use sex boldly in their music, who flaunt their bodies but who also remain insistently in charge of their mass media images, women who, like Ke$ha, sing songs with titles like "Party at a Rich Dude's House" and rap about being young, drunk, lost, and loving it? (My friend, theorist Micha Cardenas, is countering gaga feminism with her own Ke$ha feminism!) While it is easy to dismiss some of this material as just mindless pop, at the same time, we might want to look again at singers who, after all, appeal to large numbers of young female fans. Why can't these women be new figures of feminism? In the end, feminists like Faludi are committed to a reform model of feminism, to the idea of feminism as a politics built around stable definitions of (white) womanhood and as a ladies' club of influence and moral dignity. Finally, the mother-daughter bond, which for Faludi is most successfully studied in the dynamic between Elizabeth Cady Stanton and her daughter Harriet, allows, according to Faludi, for the gains of one age to be passed on to the next. But never does Faludi question whether the gains of white women in

one era actually benefit women of color in the next, or whether
the goals of white middle-class women reflect anything beyond
their race and class interests.

WHAT IF . . . ?

So, disregarding the fantasy of a peaceful transfer of knowledge
to the daughters, let's leave family, mommies, babies, and whiny
feminism behind and move onward, upward, gaga-ward. Gaga
is a hypothetical form of feminism, one that lives in between the
"what" and the "if": What if we gendered people according to
their behavior? What if gender shifted over the course of a lifetime—what if someone began life as a boy but became a boygirl
and then a boy/man? What if some males are ladies, some ladies
are butch, some butches are women, some women are gay, some
gays are feminine, some femmes are straight, and some straight
people don't know what the hell is going on? What if we live
in a world where things happen so fast that the life span, and
progress through it, looks very different than it did only two
decades ago? What if you begin life as a queer mix of desires
and impulses and then are trained to be heterosexual but might
relapse into queerness once the training wears off? What if the
very different sexual training that boys and girls receive makes
them less and less compatible? What if girls stopped wearing
pink, boys started wearing skirts, women stopped competing
with other women, and men stopped grabbing their crotches in
public? What if we actually started to notice the ways in which
race and sexuality have become hopelessly entangled with notions of the normal and the perverse, so that we could see the
ways in which the white family hides its secrets behind thick lay-
ers of presumed normativity, while black families in particular
but also Latino and Muslim families are regularly cast as excessive or intolerant, traditional and behind the times? The "what

if" is fun and hopeful but it is also serious and penetrating and might just bring us to the brink of new ideas about old topics.

In a more serious vein, what if sexual orientation could also be read as less fixed, less determined, more negotiated and fluid? What if we actually stopped and recognized the multiple ways in which men and women, boys and girls, exceed and fall short of the definitions that give those categories heft and longevity? And why should we do all this? Because despite all reasonable predictions, we live in a world that still controls girls and girl sexualities within a rigid system of blocks, taboos, and prohibitions. And we still expect boys to punish each other into "normal" forms of masculinity and then compete and agitate for female attention in ways that make women into killjoys, moral arbiters, and passive bystanders at the prom, still waiting to be asked to dance. And this early training is very misleading in the sense that, once the early courtship between men and women is complete, very often it is the woman who becomes the active partner in the relationship, bullying her male partner into marriage, childrearing, domestic responsibility, and more. Her presumed passivity has to morph quickly and definitively into a multitasking, frantic form of controlling authority. His presumed activity has to transform just as completely into a quiescent, submissive mode that makes him the sous-chef to her ratatouille. In fact, gendered adulthood nowadays often represents a total reversal of the gender roles that have been drummed into children, and this is true across ethnic groups and classes. In fact, it is well known that as an industrial economy has given way to a service economy, and especially in the economic downturn of the early twenty-first century, women have done better economically than men, so much so that in many households, women are the main wage earners.

There are many different versions of the female-headed household—in working-class households, particularly black households, many men have been incarcerated within an increasingly unfair system of justice that penalizes men of color for petty crimes while exonerating white businessmen for bankrupting the nation. Female-headed households are also found among white middle-class communities, often because, even when men are present, they are un- or underemployed. Or, more worryingly, they choose not to work and think of themselves as "artists," "poets," "musicians," as dreamers who are so alternative, they are cool enough to let their wives bring home the bacon while they make a bit of cash here or there through their "art." Academic women, it turns out, according to my own very informal poll, are particularly susceptible to these new, alternative forms of masculinity—many female academics and female professionals in general are supporting men who have chosen not to grow up, not to take economic responsibility for others, and who are happy to give up on the rat race of actually making a living. They do all this, by the way, often without taking on extra responsibility for domestic labor.

The excessive training that we give to boys and girls to transform them from anarchic, ungendered blobs into gender automatons, then is (a) dangerous, and (b) not necessary, and (c) not actually consistent with lived reality. And as some girls grow up to become anorexics and some boys grow up to become bullies, many girls grow up to be overachieving micromanagers, and many boys grow up to be underachieving slackers, yet we still refuse to give up on the models of masculinity and femininity that have been established as ordinary and normal and good. And we spend very little time, relatively speaking, attending to the problems with this model of heterosexuality and figuring out how to fix them.

In university gender-studies classes, heterosexuality gets scant treatment, mostly because we all assume that we know all too well how heterosexuality works and, therefore, by the same logic, what we really need to teach and learn about are all the fringe sexualities that become the targets for homophobic and transphobic policies and attitudes. When I taught an Introduction to Gender and Sexuality class, this was very much the approach I took. As a queer person, and a gender-queer person whose gender was indeterminate on a good day, I became exhibit A in the freak show that the class became. Every week, a mostly heterosexual lecture hall would be treated to fascinating information about gays, lesbians, transgender people, intersexuality, and so on, but the students would rarely be asked to think about how this information affected them and their own sexualities. And so, a couple of years ago, tired of being on show, I began teaching the same course, Introduction to Gender and Sexuality, as How on Earth Does Heterosexuality Work? OK, it was not actually called that, but that was the basic message of the class from start to finish. Using clips from *Desperate Housewives*, *The Sopranos*, *The Bachelor*, and other TV shows, I would act like an anthropologist visiting a strange group of people engaged in odd sexual rituals, showing the class what heterosexuality looked like from the outside.

In many ways, the "How weird is that?" approach to heterosexuality in the context of gender studies works much better than the "Try to be tolerant of these weirdos" approach showcasing queerness. It forces the very students who are deeply invested in norms, their own and other people's, to face the music and look at their own investments, their own issues, their own struggles with what is supposed to come naturally. The focus on the strangeness of heterosexuality allowed us to think through eating disorders as a vicious side effect of adolescent misogyny; it forced men in the class to ask themselves about their own relations to masculinity, to other men, to women, and to homophobia. And it led women to notice the significant differences

between the ways in which they developed peer relations with
other women (friendships often focused on food, clothes, and
boys), and the ways men developed peer relations with other
men (friendships focused on male bonding, drinking, and sports,
but rarely stemming from long discussions about girls).

In these classes, I also used the example of pornography, not
to berate men for turning their attention away from their flesh-
and-blood partners and directing it toward online sexual imagery, but rather to reveal the stark differences in outcome of the
sexual training of boys and girls. While girls experience sexual
awakenings largely in the context of the matrices of prohibitions
that I described earlier, and while in most girls desire is never actually given a chance to flow and weave itself around objects and
fetishes, boys are quickly encouraged and incited to feel desire,
to direct that desire, to indulge desire. Pornographic archives
suggest the range and the depth of male sexual imaginaries
(Chicks with dicks! Fat chicks! Muscle chicks! Hairy chicks!),
and women's magazines illustrate the narrowness and restriction
of female sexual imaginaries (10 things he really wants sexually
but is afraid to tell you . . . 10 ways to please your man . . . 10
ways to be a complete and utter bimbo so as not to threaten
your boyfriend and make him lose his mojo). While not all pornography is for men, and not all women's magazines are read
by women, what we call "men" and "women" are bodies that
have generally been trained in either the interruption of desire
(women) or its free flow (men). By the time heterosexual romance begins, the formula of male persuasion and female defer-
ral, male solicitations and female refusals, male randiness and
female frigidity, has already established a large part of the male-
female sexual script. And as men and women age, heterosexuality requires all kinds of aids to maintain this formula—Viagra
for men and plastic surgeries for women.

Again, none of this is to say that these stereotypes of heterosexual conduct are installed across all boys and all girls; just to note that the training we give men and women pushes each partner into very different relations to sex and to their bodies. The anthropologist of sexuality, Gayle Rubin, in fact, noted astutely several decades ago that there has been a long history of training women's sexuality via the mechanism of restraint. In an extremely influential essay that tried to account for the production of the meaning of "male" and "female" in precapitalist and capitalist societies, Rubin noted that the meaning of "woman" in early human societies emerged out of the tendency of tribes and groups to create bonds with one another through the exchange of women.[5] This "traffic in women" then established the meaning of womanhood within a system of "institutionalized heterosexuality," and kinship rested upon the circulation of women between and among men within a set of taboos (incest, homosexuality) and according to a set of obligatory forms (reproductive heterosexuality). As Rubin summarized neatly: "Kinship systems dictate some sculpting of the sexuality of both sexes."[6] She continues: "It would be in the interests of the smooth and continuous operation of such a system if the woman in question did not have too many ideas of her own about whom she might want to sleep with. From the standpoint of the system, the preferred female sexuality would be one which responded to the desires of others, rather than one which actively desired and sought a response."[7] Now, of course, we are a long way from "bridewealth," dowries, and the traffic in women, but the system of sexualities and genders that preceded capitalism and turned women into a form of currency did not, contrary to expectations, simply fade away once wage labor came into the picture and offered women ways of earning their own living. In fact, capitalism also made claims on women, claims that required them to perform domestic tasks for free, for example, and capitalism also benefited from a compliant female sexuality.

Capitalism also benefits, as I implied earlier, from the control of children's sexuality, and in the United States, we control children's sexuality to the point of making their budding desires less sources of pleasure and more vectors for abuse. As Judith Levine claims in the title of her brave and controversial book, protecting kids from sex is "harmful to minors."[8] Rather than confirming the popular opinion that access to sex can be damaging to kids, Levine leverages evidence of media-fueled panics about child abductions, satanic rituals, and pedophilia to show that holding back information from children about abortion, sexual experimentation, and contraception has had a disastrous impact on several generations of American kids and their parents. Levine argues, in gaga feminist style, that conservative and often religious-based panics over any and all signs of sexuality in children have dire consequences. As she puts it, a zealous watchfulness in relation to child sexual expression has contributed to a "gradual pathologizing of normative children's sexuality," and, accordingly, what we even mean by normal behavior gets pushed "a few notches to the right."[9]

Levine is rightfully wary of the term "normal," especially when it cozies up to its twin concept "natural," and she works hard to reveal how, where, and when our understanding of the normal gets manufactured, repurposed, recirculated, and then leveraged for the purposes of control. All these mechanisms that constrict and constrain children's desires become part of the equation of what they actually like to do sexually later on. In many ways, there is no innocent intervention when it comes to sex. Sexuality is a kind of spongy life force: it absorbs all information, good and bad, it becomes saturated even by the material it is supposed to repel, and in fact, the presumably repellant material just becomes the foundation for other, more resilient, modes of desire. Levine, by asking impertinent questions about children and sex—like, Why label a child a victim if she doesn't feel victimized? or, Why presume that all sexual conduct between adults and children is unwanted by the child or that all sexual activity among kids under the age of ten is pernicious?—has pushed back on one version of feminism that sees women and girls perpetually as the victims of unchecked male sexual aggression, and has pushed forward with another that understands children as sexual, parents as erotic figures, and sexuality itself as the pursuit of pleasure. By casting "harm" in terms of the judgments adults pass about child sexuality rather than in terms of exposure to inappropriate material, Levine went gaga and began a much-needed public conversation about the folly of imposing sexual regulation on children and the wisdom of making more-neutral assessments about what children want. Indeed, Levine proposed, when we really don't know or understand what children want or how they may feel about something, we could always do something wacky and crazy . . . like asking them to let us know what feels good and what feels intrusive or wrong.

So, while child sexuality is denied, male sexuality encouraged, female sexuality repressed, and religious leaders are given free hand with the legislation of desire, gaga feminism proposes to join forces with the kind of sexual liberation proposed by Judith Levine and Gayle Rubin before her. If we can figure out how to stop policing children's sexuality, we might also be closer to understanding how to disrupt the transmission of moralistic and inadequate narratives of sex, love, and marriage from one generation to the next. Rubin showed us how female passivity and sexual submission actually carried over from precapitalist societies to industrial capitalist ones. But the lingering question is why so little changes in the male-female dynamic when so

much else ebbs and flows around it. As we go from analog to
digital, from local to global, from proximity to virtuality, from
community to social network, how is it that we can shift and
alter our perceptions of so many of the building blocks of social
life but we still cling to practically nineteenth-century notions
of the intimate, the domestic, and the private? Now, I am not at
all saying that nothing has changed or that marriage cultures are
the same now as they ever were; obviously we can chart massive
shifts in the meaning of sexual contact as we move from, say,
personal ads to online dating services. And we can also see that
notions of friendship, coupledom, and even family have shifted
somewhat to accommodate the collisions of personal and re-
mote, private and public that occur on millions of computer
screens every night around the world. And yet . . . and yet,
as we entered a new century, mobile devices firmly in hand,
we did not choose to dial up a brand-new world of connection, instead we began to ask whether we could expand the old
world of marriage to accommodate more people and whether
we could extend the old notion of family to include more and
more intricate relations. This is akin to old episodes of *Star
Trek*, in which we are seen to have traveled years and miles
from earth, we are in completely new solar systems, and yet,
when aliens appear, they still take the form of men and women
and follow heterosexual modes of intimacy. A few wavy lines
on the forehead or an extra nose or something signals difference, but the actual scripting of human sexual relations is left
completely untouched.

A few illustrations of the way the persistence of old models
of gender hampers the development of new ones might be helpful
here. In mainstream cinema, the representation of heterosexual
romance seems hardly to change at all despite massive changes in
the real world. Just as little girls are sold extremely manipulative

narratives about princesses and unicorns at age five (or they get "eaten" by Cinderella, as the title of Peggy Orenstein's 2011 book has it),[10] by age fifteen, they are offered the "chick flick" by way of compensation for the disappointments that are sure to follow from the realizations that the childhood narratives about romantic trysts, cuddly babies, and cute puppies are about to be replaced by cheating, marriage-averse guys, the trauma of childbirth, and dog poop. (I jest, but you get the point about the distance between princes and husbands, dolls and babies, stuffed animals and animals that shit all over your carpet . . . right?)

Whoever currently writes romantic comedies, or at least whoever writes the ones not written by Nora Ephron (*You've Got Mail*, *Sleepless in Seattle*, *When Harry Met Sally*, and so on)—and it really seems to be one person or one committee of mediocre screenplay writers, given the uniformity of the genre (think *Something about Mary*, *Pretty Woman*, *Runaway Bride*, *The Proposal*, *Sweet Home Alabama*, *The Break-Up*, *Wedding Crashers* and the list goes on)—must think that (a) men and women do not really like each other but (b) they really want to get together, and (c) there is no point in getting together unless you first have a huge obstacle standing between you and your object of desire (examples: his parents, her parents, his girlfriend, her dog, his commitment phobia, her biological clock, his homosexuality, her obsession with weddings, his virginity— yes, *his*, think about it for a minute . . . Steve Carell, Catherine Keener . . . you got it!—Russell Brand, age differences, his job, her ambition, her looks, her memory loss, and so on and so forth). In fact, given how much of early life for heterosexuals involves subtle and less subtle nudges to get a mate, settle down, get married, it is kind of bewildering to see how the romantic comedy wants to, needs to, has to produce obstacles in order to make love seem hard won, worthwhile, and, well, romantic.

Romance, it seems, loves an obstacle ("The course of true love never did run smooth" as the Bard once said, prescriptively I think, rather than descriptively, given how much mileage Shakespearean comedies themselves gain out of obstacles to the marriage of the principals). For gay people, of course, obstacles are the name of the game, and they abound in the form of sanctioned and unsanctioned homophobia (You can't do that!); sexual curiosity (Why do you want to do that?); outrage (That's illegal! Please don't do that!); and disgust (Oh, must you? And in public?). But for straight people, the obstacles to true love must be created, crafted, nurtured, and then quickly discarded as soon as an hour and twenty minutes of fun has been had by all. And so a lover's family suddenly accepts the fiancé they had so quickly rejected; a lover's child finally comes around and accepts the new mate; the lover moves from the wrong love object (homosexual, superficial, commitment phobic, fantastically good-looking, or all of the above) to the right love object (putatively heterosexual, deep, caring, pretty good-looking, steady) and the rest, as they say, is history. Or, at least, the rest is Hollywood.

I will return to the recent bumper crop of romantic comedies focused on marriage (*Bride Wars*, *Bridesmaids*, *He's Just Not That Into You*) in chapter 4, and there we will also look at the romantic comedies' masculine other: the bromance. But, meanwhile, there is another new genre of films that attempts to fold itself around the new forms of white middle-class heterosexuality. While these films simply settle for the idea that when it comes to heterosexuality, the more things change, the more they stay the same, gaga feminism sees these changes as opportunities for new understandings of gendered intimacy, other versions of gendered desire, and wants to take advantage of the instability of heterosexuality, an instability born of a brave new world made up of abundantly competent women and totally incompetent men. The new genre of films that tries to make sense of this new development and contain its wild potential focuses upon redundant masculinities, and tries to recycle these useless models while building up heroic narratives around them. This genre, mumblecore, as it has been named, was represented in mainstream cinema by the 2010 film *Cyrus*, but it encompasses a whole set of both mainstream and indie films, all of which imagine themselves to be showcasing alternative masculinities while in fact they are just trying to rescue an anachronistic masculinity from the trash heap of history. In the 2009 film *Humpday*, two buddies decide to make a porno movie together while their wives/girlfriends are working real jobs. In an earlier and high-end version of mumblecore, *Little Children* (directed by Todd Field, 2006), gorgeous and talented women (played by Kate Winslet and Jennifer Connelly) are married to underachieving men who let their wives work while they pine over their lost youth or cruise the Internet for porn.

The genre is rounded out by the Judd Apatow factory of films featuring Neanderthal males and fine women, *Knocked Up* being the obvious example. In Apatow's world, sad and nerdy, out-of-shape men successfully cruise successful and ambitious beautiful women. True love, these films now tell us, can bring a lovely lady to see the charm of a crusty loser; it can allow a go-getter femme to ignore the complete lack of ambition of her geeky partner; true love lets losers win . . . as long as they are male. There is no possibility of the reverse situation becoming the foundation of romance—no lady nerds without jobs or good looks can expect Prince Charming to show up any time soon. And while women in these films, like high school students preparing for a competitive college application, pad their resumes with good works, yoga classes, advanced degrees, high salaries, and lots of know-how, their schlubby partners-to-be rest secure in the knowledge that they may not have a job, they may have no prospects of a job any time soon, they may lack good hygiene, tell few jokes, show little to no initiative, but, heterosexual love being what it is, and given the market's tilt toward male eligibility, as long as the guy has a semifunctional penis, and sometimes even if he doesn't, he will get laid!

Let's look more closely at one example of mumblecore to see what we are dealing with here. *Cyrus*—or Oedipus Wrecks—is a wretchedly weird film in which Marisa Tomei is romanced by the singularly unappealing John C. Reilly only to be thwarted in her sexual escapades when her twentysomething son, played creepily by Jonah Hill, expresses his Oedipal objections to the match. In a romantic comedy with few jokes, little romance, and a massive "ick" factor (the romantic leads meet as the man is peeing on a rosebush and his partner-to-be thinks it is cute!), so little was appealing about the film that reviewers tried to rescue it by inventing a new genre to explain this and other navel-gazing not-very-funny rom-com, sex-with-mom, ho-hum films—thus, *mumblecore.*

What these films really do is grapple unsuccessfully with many of the changes that I am charting here: when the women get smart, these films show the men riding her coattails; when the women get fed up, the films show the men playing the spinster card and reminding the women that society abhors an unmarried female. And so, if white heterosexual women become more competent, more powerful, and better paid, what happens, these films ask, to white heterosexual men who, in the past, got a lot of mileage out of being the providers, the workers, the members of the partnership who knew how to do stuff? Well, the mumblecore films provide an answer: If women become more competent, then men are relieved of their obligations to be efficient and productive. If the woman is earning well, then maybe the man can take a long break. If she can manage the household, the kids, the banking, the shopping, and their sex life, then maybe he should just kick back, put his feet up, and wait for her to tell him what to do.

Mumblecore films provide a justification for a new form of parasitical masculinity that I like to call "angler" masculinity, after the anglerfish. For those who have not read up on these crafty little creatures, male anglerfish are much smaller than the females; they can only survive by attaching to the larger female, fusing with her and mating with her. She then spawns eggs and baby fish . . . and her mate? He hangs on for dear life and feeds when she feeds. The mumblecore/angler male films by the Duplass brothers (*Cyrus*), Andrew Bujalski (*Funny Ha Ha*), but also inspired by Judd Apatow (*Knocked Up*) give this angler guy meaning—yes, he may be a loser, may lack a job, a purpose in life, ambition, charm, likeable qualities, this may all be true, but mumblecore imagines beautiful women throwing themselves at these men not despite their shortcomings but because of them. If there weren't plenty of evidence in the real world for this phenomenon of smart women/slacker men couplings, mumblecore would be truly offensive. In fact, when *Knocked Up* came out in 2007, articles began appearing in the press about slacker dude/high-ambition lady couplings. One such article in the *SF Weekly*, for example, titled "Slacker Guys and Striver Girls," looked at real-life versions of the mismatched pairs of ambitious women and stoner guys.[11] The article came to the conclusion that the slacker's days were done, because many of the women interviewed had moved on from stoner boneheads to career guys, but looking around the tabloids and seeing all the stories of famous women like Sandra Bullock and Jennifer Aniston who go out with lazy guys who cheat on them, one suspects that the slacker dude has at least one more generation

to go before he gets phased out along with the model of heterosexuality that invests in the idea that any guy who will marry
you is marriage material.

Basically, the mumblecore films expose a deeply troubling
component of the new heterosexualities described here—namely,
that there is no point blaming men alone for the breakdown
in the functionality of heterosexuality. Women carry a large
amount of responsibility for what heterosexuality has become,
and whether they are desperate housewives complaining about
male perfidy or newly divorced women bemoaning the lack of
single men their age or young women who are quickly lured by
men twice their age into sexual relations with financial benefits,
or even if they are women who dislike women, mean girls who
punish other girls to punish themselves, or women who "mas-
querade" (in the psychoanalytic terminology) or pose as incompetent in order to make their incompetent partners feel better
about themselves, however you play it, women are as much to
blame for the sad state of affairs that we call heterosexual romance as men.

This is not to make an antifeminist argument about women
being the real problem or women needing to shape up; it is,
rather, a "face the music" kind of statement about the fact that
gender hierarchies persist, at least in part, because women per-
petuate them and have learned how to benefit from them. Gaga
feminism proposes that we look more closely at heterosexuality, not simply to blame it for the continued imbalance of the
sexes but to find in its collapse new modes of intimate relation.
And this form of feminism actually imagines that men as well
as women will feel liberated by the possibilities that the end of
heterosexuality and the end of normal create.

But . . . what if we incorporate all the macro changes that
we have experienced in a few short decades into the everyday?

What if we start noticing that the families in which children grow up are far different from the families in which many of us were raised, and that those changes have often been for the better? The claustrophobia of the nuclear family was formerly only alleviated by more family, extended family, by cousins and aunts and uncles and grandparents. But now, children are apt to have many adults in their life, adults, moreover, to whom they are not even related. Of course, the expansion of the tight family circle to include nonbiologically related others has raised a kind of hysteria about pedophilia such that our freeways are littered with electronic notices about "child abduction," and milk cartons bear the sad visages of missing children. These children are often disgruntled youth who have run as far away as possible from their abusive family households, or children who have been abducted by a parent in a custody battle; only much more rarely is the child a victim of stranger abduction. More often than we think, it is the family, and not the outside world, that is the danger zone for kids. What would happen if we actually began to incorporate this version of the family into our mainstream representations?

Now, of course, there are families and "families" in the USA, and when people talk about "saving the family" or "protecting the family" or "investing in family," they generally have a white middle-class family in mind. Few of the models of the family used in mainstream politics to argue for this or against that (for stay-at-home moms; against abortion, for example) envision a black family as the family that must be saved from the breakdown of traditional gender roles or the manipulation of reproductive potential. The black family in particular has a vexed history in the United States, as so many scholars have commented, precisely because it was decimated both by slavery and by the Jim Crow period that followed.

The black family nowadays is often represented in the media as more conservative, more homophobic, but also more broken, more divided, and more perverse than any other. When gay marriage was voted down in California in the 2008 elections, for example, black voters were supposedly to blame, and the media engineered a standoff between white gay-marriage supporters and black straight-marriage defenders. Subsequent studies showed that the influence of black voters in relation to the defeat of the move to overturn Proposition 8 had been greatly exaggerated, and that black voters, even religious black voters, are much more concerned with social justice issues than with "family values": they may oppose gay marriage but not go out of their way to vote against it. In a 2011 article in *The Root*, for example, journalist David Kaufman reminded readers: "Focused far more on job creation, health care and education than on gay marriage, black voters aren't supporting conservative candidates *simply because* they oppose LGBT rights. Instead, they are voting for progressive pro-LGBT candidates—*despite disagreeing* with their pro-LGBT platforms" (emphasis in original).[12]

The divided black family has long been the target of American sociologists, as scholar Roderick Ferguson documents in his book *Aberrations in Black*.[13] Cast by sociologists and public-policy makers in the 1960s as the root cause of black poverty, the black household has been caricatured in terms of all that supposedly goes wrong when fathers are absent and mothers are too present. The myth of the powerful black matriarch and the delinquent dad has covered over the reality of the struggling single mother and the incarcerated father. Rather than looking at the reasons that so many black households struggle, conservative family discourse has chosen the easy route of blaming poverty and destitution on the breaking up of the family rather than recognizing the broken black family as part of the long arc of slavery and its aftermath.

In terms of black gay and lesbian households, queer sociologist Mignon Moore's book *Invisible Families: Gay Identities, Relationships, and Motherhood among Black Women*,[14] has shown that black gays and lesbians tend to follow many of the same patterns as heterosexual black parents and are often much more concerned with the consequences of racism and class politics than with marriage equality.

So, for all kinds of people across many different ethnicities in the United States, the family, feminism, and sex/gender norms need a major update. Gaga feminism to the rescue! Now, I am not saying that the new feminism I outline here, a feminism that recognizes multiple genders, that contributes to the collapse of our current sex-gender systems, a feminism less concerned with the equality of men and women and more interested in the abolition of these terms as such, I am not saying that gaga feminism will save anyone, or rescue any outmoded social form from total redundancy, but, in a mode of frivolity and because, for many feminists, there is really nothing left to lose, some kind of political project, whimsical or otherwise, seems to be in order. So gaga feminism will locate Lady Gaga as merely the most recent marker of the withering away of old social models of desire, gender, and sexuality, and as a channel for potent new forms of relation, intimacy, technology, and embodiment.

I am sure you are now wondering—can anyone be a gaga feminist? The short answer is—yes! The long answer is—no. Technically speaking, anyone can be a gaga feminist, but practically speaking, many people will not want to be. Gaga feminism, after all, wants to incite people to go gaga, to give up on the tried and the true, the real and the authentic, the proven and the tested, and instead encourages a move toward the insane, the preposterous, the intellectually loony and giddy, hallucinatory visions of alternative futures.

Gaga feminism is not something to which you will subscribe; you will not sign up for it, you will not vote for it. Instead, it is something you will do, something you can practice, something to be. And by the way, contrary to Lady Gaga's own manifesto, you will not be born a gaga feminist, "Born This Way," you will, to quote an earlier gaga feminist, Simone de Beauvoir, become one. Gaga feminism will be a way of seeing new realities that shadow our everyday lives—gaga feminists will see multiple genders, finding male/female dichotomies to be outdated and illogical. Gaga feminism is a gender politics that recognizes the ways in which our ideas of the normal or the acceptable depend completely upon racial and class-based assumptions about the right and the true; gaga feminism will abandon the norm the way a hiker might throw out her compass—once the compass has been lost, every direction is right, every path seems attractive, and getting lost becomes both a possibility and a pleasure. Think of gaga feminism in the same way that Lady Gaga thinks of clothes—not as functional and utilitarian but as utopian and visionary. When Lady Gaga wears a meat dress or five-inch heels, she does so to call attention to the whimsy of personhood, the ways in which we all need to see each other anew, find new surfaces, name those surfaces differently, and confuse the relations between surface and depth.

Obviously any movement that calls itself "feminist" must assume some privileged relation to the category of "woman," and gaga feminism is not different in that respect. But what I mean by "woman" in this book will always be subject to contextual definitions. And gaga feminism may begin with questions of concern to bodies gendered as female, but it ends by recognizing that gender concerns all bodies, all genders, and a new gaga gender politics requires a thorough recalibration of the ways in which we know, recognize, and value each other's genders, desires, and embodiments.

If I had to lay out some basic principles of gaga feminism, a few rules to guide you as you contemplate this new, gaga wave of feminist frenzy, they might look something like this:

1. Wisdom lies in the unexpected and the unanticipated—to recognize new forms of politics, social structures, and personhood, we really have to take some big leaps into the unknown. Going gaga means letting go of many of your most basic assumptions about people, bodies, and desires.

2. Transformation is inevitable, but don't look for the evidence of change in the everyday; look around, look on the peripheries, the margins, and there you will see its impact. Let me explain—as every good baseball fan knows, when a player hits a long ball, you cannot tell if it is a home run by following the arc of the ball itself. You have to look into the stands and see whether the fans are on their feet waiting to catch the fly ball or whether they are seated and following the ball's flight into a well-placed glove. In other words, don't watch the ball, watch the crowd.

3. Think counterintuitively, act accordingly. A lot of what we learn as "common sense" actually makes no sense, especially as change does happen in complex societies such as the ones we inhabit. The notion that parents should "stay together for the children," for example, makes no sense when that entails having children live under the same roof as parents who hate each other. The idea that divorce is a terrible thing and that kids need two parents, one male and one female, preferably living

together, is also debatable. Many kids now grow up in divided households, and they experience that division as a kind of liberation from nuclearity. When things are not going too well in one household, they can take refuge in the other. When dynamics get difficult with one set of parents, they can take a break with the other. What is intuitive for one generation becomes an obstacle to change for the next. Nothing lasts forever, and common sense needs to twist and turn in the winds of change.

4. Practice creative nonbelieving. I know it is not fashionable nowadays to be antireligious. We have reached a kind of "live and let live" sensibility when it comes to religiosity and spirituality and all that stuff. But when it comes to gender norms and sexual mores, religion really is the root of all evil, and that cuts across many religions. This is a bit of a problem for a branch of feminism that calls itself gaga feminism and takes Lady Gaga as a kind of mascot. She is, of course, like Madonna, thoroughly saturated in Catholic imagery and narratives of sacrifice, virgin/whore oppositions, and Judas-like betrayals. All the more reason, then, for this feminist, this gaga feminist, to flag some of the differences between Lady Gaga and gaga feminism from the get-go—religion is a no-no and God has got to go-go. Christianity in particular has not been held properly accountable for all of the violence and misery that it has brought upon the world through its missions, morality, and miserable notions of salvation. As an anti-Christian doctrine, gaga feminism will not be your salvation, it will not save you or redeem you, it will not forgive you for your sins, but instead it encourages you to be a nonbeliever, and to keep your spiritual beliefs to yourself.

5. Finally, gaga feminism is outrageous. This is not a feminism for the faint of heart nor for the weak of knees . . . this is a feminism that has no truck with shame or embarrassment, it is for the freaks and geeks, the losers and failures, the kids who were left out at school, the adults who still don't fit in. This is not a new social networking tool, nor a way to win friends and influence people. Gaga feminism is impolite, abrupt, abrasive, and bold. To be a feminist, you have to go gaga!

No, but seriously, folks, gaga feminism will not give you rules, will not lead you to the promised land. It may not even make your life better. But gaga feminism exists already in small random acts by gaga people who are improvising revolution right now in ways that may startle you into a new awareness of the change that is happening all around. This feminism is not about sisterhood, motherhood, sorority, or even women. It is about shifting, changing, morphing, extemporizing political positions quickly and effectively to keep up with the multimedia environments in which we all live and to stay apace of what some have called "the coming insurrection." Here and now, our reality is being rescripted, reshot, reimagined, and if you don't go gaga soon, you may wake up and find that you have missed the future and become the past.

TWO

Gaga Genders

Fathers are biological necessities, but social accidents.

—Margaret Mead

MALE PREGNANCY

When Oprah needed a ratings boost a couple of years ago, she engineered the TV-talk-show equivalent of the moon walk: she found a pregnant man, Thomas Beatie, to come on her show and talk about his experience with carrying a child, his impending fatherhood, and his battles with a medical system not equipped to handle male pregnancies. The story took off immediately, and while right-wing TV hosts delighted in sneering at and decrying the media spectacle that sprang up overnight around a pregnant trans-man and his girlfriend, queer communities were at first quietly stunned by the sudden publicity of unorthodox reproduction and then not so quietly irritated that the pregnant man, Beatie, was claiming to be the very first trans man ever to bear a child. Beatie's claim came as a surprise to quite a few other transgender men who, over the past decade, have transitioned without having hysterectomies and then gone off hormones for a while to get pregnant and bear children. Patrick Califia and his boyfriend, Matt Rice, for example, were quite public about having a baby after they had both transitioned from female to male. Patrick went off hormones for a while and was pregnant, but didn't appear in *People* magazine or on *Oprah* to inform everyone. The question of who got there first, of course, misses the point: the pregnant man should be seen less as an individual phenomenon and more as an indication that a new politics of reproduction has emerged, with all kinds of unforeseen consequences.

In the middle of "the year of the pregnant man," I fielded numerous calls from journalists and media people, wanting an interview with me that would help explain the meaning of this seemingly miraculous development to an interested but confused audience. I found myself oddly flummoxed by the whole thing—I didn't want to add to the voyeuristic sensationalism surrounding this rather unremarkable occurrence (unremarkable because it is not so extraordinary to transition to male from female while holding on to one's reproductive bits), but I did want to correct some of the misinformation about transgenderism that was circulating alongside the "gee whiz" stories about male reproductive potential. I didn't want to give any of the homophobic journalists ammunition for their hateful stories, but I also didn't want to contribute to the emergent mythology that saw Thomas Beatie as a brave pioneer, a one-of-a-kind phenomenon, and a leading player in the reorganization of the family. In fact, while I would say one thing about Beatie to queer audiences, I might say something quite different to straight ones. To a queer audience, I would try to create a conversation about media manipulation, about the possibility that Beatie was just trying to make a bit of cash by staging his pregnancy as a kind of circus or sideshow. But to straight interlocutors, I would talk about the mechanics of sex-reassignment surgeries, the in-between status of so many bodies, the gender flexibility that is an increasing part of our sense of embodiment, and the new arrangements of the familial and the parental that continue to emerge in the wake of IVF technologies.

It was a difficult set of conversations to switch between, and at least one TV station sent a camera crew to interview me and then decided not to use the footage because I wasn't telling a simple and coherent story. I was muddying the waters when they felt a desire for clarity, raising questions when they wanted answers. While the puerile Fox News shock jocks wanted to resolve the question of the pregnant transgender man using the playground method of chortling and finger-pointing, the "look at the freak" mode of dispelling uncomfortable material so favored by male adolescents and conservative Christians, the liberal press wanted the pregnant man to mark some clear advancement in human society, but somehow could not name either the cause or the effect of such progress. Queer commentators, meanwhile, were sanguine about the materiality of the pregnant male body, unsurprised by its sudden emergence, but often suspicious of Beatie's motivations. As the story receded to the back of the tabloid magazines, I waited for the student papers to appear, be they by undergraduates gawking at this "stranger than fiction" story or by earnest graduate students sure they had stumbled across the very symbol they needed to prove the end of everything or the beginning of something else. I still have very little to say about the pregnant man per se, and even less interest in reading another word about him, be it in a book, a magazine, a dissertation, or a C-grade essay, but I do think of Thomas Beatie as a convenient marker of some seismic shifts that seem to have occurred below the surface of our seemingly rigid and frozen gender and sexuality systems.

Many a feminist career has been launched with predictions about the brave new world that could rise from the dust of contemporary gender norms with the right technological innovations. Not all of these predictions have been utopian, and indeed many have been profoundly dystopian, in the *Stepford Wives* vein of imagining the control of female bodies through the imposition of placid, docile mannequins made to have sex, clean, cook, and reproduce. In 1970, Shulamith Firestone made her own bold predictions, and they proved to be highly prescient: Firestone was a radical feminist prophet for some, a madwoman for others, but she was recognized even in the mainstream press as a relevant critic who used Marxist theory to approach "the woman question." Firestone predicted that when reproductive technologies became available to all women, many women would choose not to bear babies but would happily cede that privilege to the medical lab. And when that day came, according to Firestone, a feminist revolution would occur, because women would be freed from the old adage that "anatomy is destiny," and the equality of the sexes would finally be possible. She wrote:

> Just as the end goal of socialist revolution was not only the elimination of the economic class *privilege* but of the economic class *distinction* itself, so the end goal of feminist revolution must be, unlike that of the first feminist movement, not just the elimination of male privilege but of the sex *distinction* itself: genital differences between human beings would no longer matter culturally. (A reversion to an unobstructed *pansexuality*—Freud's "polymorphous perversity"— would probably supersede hetero/homo/bi-sexuality.) The reproduction of the species by one sex for the benefit of both would be replaced by (at least the option of) artificial reproduction: children would be born to both sexes equally, or independently of either, however one chooses to look at it; the dependence of the child on the mother (and vice versa) would give way to a greatly shortened dependence on a small group of others in general, and any remaining inferiority to adults in physical strength would be compensated for culturally. The division of labour would be ended by the elimination of labour altogether (through cybernetics). The tyranny of the biological family would be broken.[1]

In this passage, we can see the future revolution unfolding before us along the lines of the trajectory that Marxists had plotted for socialist revolution. So while socialists wanted to eliminate economic distinctions that in turn produce rich and poor people and indeed make some people's wealth dependent upon the poverty of others, so the feminist revolution would eliminate gender distinctions based upon biological functions that then socially dictated parental functions. Where reproduction becomes artificial, male and female distinctions and mother and father roles wither away, leaving in their place only parents; and if we create machines to do our labor for us too, then we rid ourselves of gendered and economic divisions of labor, and we lose the rationale for the biological family completely.

Firestone was a central player in a left-leaning branch of radical feminism that understood gender relations to be at the very heart of social transformation, rather than the afterthought to which so many socialist movements had relegated them. Like a Karl Marx in flowing feminist clothing, she was sure that the march of history would create the conditions under which revolution could occur. For her, with the right historical configurations of technology, political readiness, and imagination, women could rise up and lose the chains that bound them to marriage and childrearing and kept them out of the professional labor market. Firestone did not foresee the pregnant man, needless to say, nor did she predict lesbian moms or dyke daddies, but she was correct in predicting that when shifts occur in the realm of reproductive technologies, social change is inevitable.

Women, Firestone asserted, have been defined by their maternal potential and forced to secure protection and support from men for their reproductive years, leading to an uneven bond of dependency. However, because this dependence seems natural or at least organic to the reproductive process, it has also seemed fixed and unchangeable. For Firestone, Marxism analogically provides an inspirational model of transformation for feminism because it casts history as process and change, not as a series of fixed and inevitable events. In other words, since things change in relation to one another, dialectically, that is, then shifts in one arena necessitate shifts in other arenas: new industrial technologies change the meaning of work, change the definitions of masculinity and femininity, alter class systems, and transform the relations between capital and commodities. Similarly, changes in reproductive technology change the meaning of biology, shift the expression and significance of embodied gender, and alter the contours of the family.

Firestone, unlike many of her feminist contemporaries—people like Andrea Dworkin, Mary Daly, and Robin Morgan, women who believed in the essence of womanhood and wanted to build a new world based upon female principles—argued for the contingency of gender dualism and saw its emergence as a function of historical and not biological necessity. We now have the means, Firestone says, due to technological innovation and human evolution, to change the way the family works and comes into being, and so change we must. Finally, Firestone urges feminists to take advantage of the technological breakthroughs in fertility and change the structures of the family that have been so disadvantageous to women. The family, she says, extends the subjugation of women that originates in their reproductive role. Change the status of that role and the family that gives it meaning and you can change all of society.

Well, needless to say, Firestone's message ultimately fell on deaf ears, and she was quickly shunted off to the fringes of feminism. As Marxism fell out of favor in the Cold War years, moreover, theories of Marxist and socialist feminism lost credibility. And as for Firestone herself, by the late 1980s she had been hospitalized several times for mental illness, and she, along with her radical ideas, was cast aside by a society not ready for either grand-scale change or its analysis.

While her society dubbed her crazy, like many people whom we designate as mentally ill, Firestone was a visionary. But prophetic as she may have been, she couldn't have foreseen the way that so much could change and yet remain the same. Here we are living in an age of artificial reproduction, a time when many women seek and receive medical assistance in becoming pregnant or finding a surrogate mother to carry their embryos; a time when shopping at a sperm bank is common enough to give rise to anxieties about incest occurring between babies born of anonymous fathers. And yet, the pull of those gender divisions that were supposed to wither away remains strong, as does the gender binary that supposedly depends upon reproductive function. This is a great moment to revisit the propositions laid out by Firestone, the ideas she advanced about the dependence of gender roles upon an ossified but wrongheaded set of connections between reproduction and nature. If we are now living in the age that Firestone predicted, could it be that we have in fact begun the arduous process of changing our understanding of sex roles and bringing them more in line with lived reality?

A slew of recent films about women making the decision to have babies independent of a romantic involvement with a man indicate that perhaps there have been some significant transformations in the way we connect biology, reproduction, and gender roles. But while the technology may be advanced, the accompanying ideologies of parenthood remain primeval. Let's take the example of one film about a woman who decides to put the horse before the carriage and have a baby independent of finding a husband. The 2010 film *The Switch* (directed by Josh Gordon and Will Speck) features Jennifer Aniston as Kassie, a forty-year-old would-be mom who just has not found the right man. When she confides in her best friend, Wally (Jason Bateman), that she is going to get pregnant, he immediately thinks she is asking him for his sperm. In fact, she finds a donor online, and then has a fertility party for the insemination rite and invites the donor to attend. Once the donor, Roland (Patrick Wilson), deposits his stuff in a cup and leaves it tactfully in the bathroom, the celebrations begin and everyone gets very drunk. Including and especially Wally, who, in a fit of jealousy, manages to spill Roland's seed in the bathroom and then, panicked and possessive, replaces it with his own. Improbably, Kassie gets pregnant! And so the fun begins.

The Switch wants to acknowledge the complications of contemporary romance and family but somehow can't extricate itself from the sticky mess of biological family. Despite the fact that Kassie leaves New York and Wally behind once she is pregnant, she returns some seven years later with little Wally—or Sebastian—in tow and, miraculously, Wally and Sebastian find themselves drawn to each other by that mysterious blood bond. Kassie, thinking that Roland is the father, begins dating him. Wally, knowing that *he* is the father, begins hanging out with Sebastian, and Sebastian, not knowing who his father may be, tells stories about one he's invented. Ultimately, of course, Kassie and Wally, despite having had zero chemistry, end up together. Roland proves to be a twit. And Sebastian is delighted to have a real family and not be, horror of horrors, the sad son of a lesbian mum (which is what his friends at school think he is). The film begins with an interesting premise about female reproductive independence, in other words, but ends with a deeply conservative and cowardly narrative about the mysteriously magnetic qualities of blood that draw biologically related people together and knit them into perfect little families.

The Switch, like other romantic comedies organized around turkey-baster reproduction, such as Jennifer Lopez's film *The Back-up Plan* (also 2010) and *Baby Mama* (2008), starring Tina Fey as an infertile career woman who hires a surrogate (Amy Poehler) and then moves her into her house, offers up the new spectacle of go-getter women wanting jobs, babies, and self-determination only to contain that vision within a new set of prescriptions for women that push them back to "natural" bonds and modes of reproduction and that simultaneously try to center the role of men, fathers, and male power. These films also all dance around the "lesbian thing," especially *Baby Mama*, raising lesbianism as a joke but then casting a sexual relationship between the two women as impossible, unthinkable, and ultimately unmentionable. Given how close the connection actually is in US culture between sperm banks, artificial insemination, and a lesbian baby boom, the specter of lesbianism continues to haunt these comedies despite the explicit rejections of lesbianism within the plots themselves. And the comedies are also hiding another, possibly more disturbing subtext, namely the idea that men are no longer necessary participants in the whole love, marriage, and reproduction process.

In fact, despite these films' insistence that men *do* matter, fathers *are* important, and that nature favors families, they are in competition with another set of images that remind us that the new reproductive politics almost relieve men of the burdens of family and reproductive responsibility altogether and in doing so make men seem . . . well, like an afterthought!

As women assume more and more of the responsibility for rearing children, men take on less and sit in the wings, watching the drama of reproduction unfold without them. And as men become lesser players in this human drama, narratives about an epidemic of single women crowd the media. In 2007, the *New*

York Times ran a telling headline: "51% of Women Now Living without Spouse." The article that followed told us that, for the first time in history, "more American women are living without a husband than with one." The reasons given for this new trend were multiple—women marry later, they live with partners but don't marry them, men die younger, high rates of divorce find many women choosing not to remarry, and so on. The article also quoted William H. Frey, a demographer with the Brookings Institution, as saying: "For better or worse, women are less dependent on men or the institution of marriage. Younger women understand this better, and are preparing to live longer parts of their lives alone or with nonmarried partners. For many older boomer and senior women, the institution of marriage did not hold the promise they might have hoped for, growing up in an 'Ozzie and Harriet' era."[2] This article was notable for its refusal of any tone of panic or tragedy in interpreting these facts. Instead, the message conveyed by the new research, the experts consulted, and the women interviewed for the piece was that marriage was not such a big loss in the end and that many women end up much happier living alone and raising their children without a man.

Of course, while many white women are choosing to be single and to live alone, for many black women, the same census reports tell us, marriage is simply not an option given the lack of available men of color and the continued racial divide in the United States that works against an increase in interracial marriages. So, while utilizing the sperm bank and the fertility clinic is largely a trend among wealthy white women, other factors contribute to massive shifts in US households for women of color. In fact, the US Census of 2010 showed that among African Americans, the share of households headed by single women now exceeds those with married couples, and a large percentage of these black female–headed households also struggle with food, poverty, and housing issues.

These new narratives about female independence, then, tend to be white, because it is white women who see single mother-hood as an opportunity rather than a burden. But white men may be responding to this trend with some measure of anxiety. In fact, the new sense of agency that some wealthy white women access through managing their own reproductive futures sepa-rate from male partners could very easily and often does give rise to a host of male anxieties about redundancy.

THE END OF MEN

As far back as 1997, we can find mainstream narratives about the disappearance of fatherhood as an institution. The winning British comedy about the disastrous economic impact of the Thatcher era upon the lives of working people, *The Full Monty* (1997), centered upon exactly such concerns and showed how shifts in the postindustrial workplace that favor women's em-ployment over men's raises the uncomfortable question of the purpose of the male body. One man warns his buddies that they are all in danger of becoming redundant—both at work and at home. As working-class employment shifted from manual to ser-vice labor and as women acquired access to IVF technologies, men, the film offers humorously, could become obsolete—"like dinosaurs," one chap adds helpfully.

More recent films confront the future that *The Full Monty* predicted, by depicting men living out their fears of obsolescence by trying to reinvent themselves, much as they did in *The Full Monty*, as sex objects for women. So, if we turn to *Roger Dodger* (2002, directed by Dylan Kidd), for example, we are offered long speeches from a wily playboy, Roger, about the "end of men." Played capably by Campbell Scott, Roger is a "ladies man," an

advertising copywriter who is good at his job and sleeping with
Joyce, his boss, played by the luminescent Isabella Rossellini. In
the film's opening scene, a table of coworkers and Roger's teenage nephew, Christopher, visiting from out of town, are listening
to Roger explain why the future of men may be limited, to say
the least. To punctuate this fantasy, Joyce is wearing a suit and
tie. The other men at the table seem meek and ineffectual and
the women are lapping up the concept of male redundancy. In a
speech that combines some shaky concepts from evolution and
genetics, Roger argues that men need to make themselves useful
because, genetically speaking, they are not necessary: "Every cell
in the human body contains a copy of the genome pattern. The
only reason sperm cells have all the fun is that up until now . . .
they were the only ones with access. Within Christopher's lifetime, artificial insemination . . . will render sperm as useless as
an assembly line worker in Detroit."

Roger goes on to argue that for women, pleasure and reproduction have always been separate, since the clitoris is outside
the vagina and since the woman does not need to have an orgasm to get pregnant. In his dystopic future, women will evolve
separately from men and will grow longer clitorises and have an
increased capacity for self-stimulation. As artificial insemination
replaces intercourse, the utility of men will fade and disappear.
Roger really should have footnoted Shulamith Firestone here and
given her credit for his rather long-winded speech, but of course,
he is not taking a feminist angle on male redundancy, he is leading up to a seduction play, a move within which he will cast men
as unnecessary only to make himself seem like no threat at all as
he makes his predatory, amorous moves on women.

He pontificates, still with nary a nod to Firestone: "The species is not static. We're in a constant state of flux. Two genders has been the default setting for one reason only: So far it's

been the only way to propagate the race." Of course, once the movie has put this neat reading of gender futurity into circulation, it doesn't know what to do with it. So the film moves quickly from a lesson in gender binarism to a workshop in sexual conquest in which Roger tries to teach his sixteen-year-old nephew Christopher (Jesse Eisenberg) how to pick up women. As Christopher quickly finds out, not only do women listen to Roger, they actually fall for his patter, and while he finds his uncle slightly embarrassing, some women actually respond well to his overtures. And when they don't? In the well-worn tradition of construction-site whistles, if the lady is not flattered by you hooting at her, then she must be a bitch or maybe she is not so good looking after all. The advances quickly turn to abuse, in other words, whenever Roger faces rejection.

This narrative comes back around in a 2011 film, *Crazy, Stupid, Love,* where Steve Carell plays a nerdy husband, Cal, who has been kicked out by his wife, Julianne Moore, and retreats to a singles bar to try his luck. Once there he watches in awe and horror as a ladies man, Jacob, played by Ryan Gosling, picks up one woman after another with just a bit of light banter and a quick "Wanna get out of here?" Jacob takes pity on Cal and teaches him the art of seduction (a well-fitting jacket, a focus on *her* in conversation, superficial banter, and a smooth hand to the small of the back at the right moment). Once Cal has learned the art, he picks up women but still sneaks by his old house at night to watch his family getting along fine without him. In *Crazy, Stupid, Love,* as in most of these films, the threatening story about redundant men is softened by a love-conquers-all narrative in which men may not be necessary but, hey, we love 'em anyway! *Crazy, Stupid, Love* also embellishes this narrative by creating a kind of "all in the family" round-robin of dating within which every "anonymous" contact that any of the men make turns out to be someone far too close to them for comfort—Cal's pickup ends up being his kid's teacher; Jacob's girlfriend is, unbeknownst to any of them, Cal's daughter; Cal's teenage son is in love with the babysitter, who is in love with Cal, and so on. It is as if we were in a small, very small, town, or a Mormon cult (more on this to come) where every romantic prospect is somehow already related to you. This is not just incest; this is super-incest! And through it all, even as the men stumble, bumble, and collapse, fail to be good husbands, boyfriends, or sons, these films raise, only to dispatch quickly, the question of whether men are necessary.

If the first round of "do we need men?" movies and commentaries followed hard on the heels of deindustrialization and post-Fordist economies, this new version of the question arises out of the ashes of what Naomi Klein has called, in *The Shock Doctrine*, "disaster capitalism," or an economic system that creates disasters in order to exploit their aftermath. Blaming a deadly combination of free-market enterprise, unchecked military spending, and the production of crises and terror as a means of coaxing citizens into giving up more and more freedom, Klein anatomizes the ways in which the George W. Bush regime led the United States to the brink of economic collapse while making many of that regime's inner circle very, very rich. She writes:

> The American Society of Civil Engineers said in 2007 that the US had fallen so far behind in maintaining its public infrastructure—roads, bridges, schools, dams—that it would take more than a trillion and a half dollars over five years to bring it back up to standard. Instead, these types of expenditures are being cut back. At the same time, public infrastructure around the world is facing unprecedented stress, with hurricanes, cyclones, floods and forest fires

all increasing in frequency and intensity. It's easy to imagine a future in which growing numbers of cities have their frail and long-neglected infrastructures knocked out by disasters and then are left to rot, their core services never repaired or rehabilitated. The well-off, meanwhile, will withdraw into gated communities, their needs met by privatized providers.[3]

Along these lines, while wealthy (mostly white) families are paying private fertility clinics to help them conceive, many immigrant families and families of color are left with no way of supporting the families they have. And as the Religious Right blames gays and lesbians, loose morals, and unchecked reproduction among poorer people for the decline of marriage and family, conservatives fail to take notice of the new forms of family and the new modes of social intimacy that have developed in the wake of the traditional family.

In the decade following the 9/11 attacks on the World Trade Center, the United States, in policies begun under George W. Bush and Vice President Dick Cheney, has fought military and cultural wars at home and abroad and has managed to scare people back into conventional sex/gender arrangements that no longer work and that do not correspond well to the economic climate that disaster capitalism has left in its wake. One small symptom of the impact of economic collapse on social relations can be identified as the reappearance of liberal feminist polemics announcing the "end of men." It was Susan Faludi, in fact, who, in her 2007 book *The Terror Dream*, most trenchantly identified a growing obsession with manhood and Wild West–style vengeance as part of the national reaction to 9/11.[4] Horrified by the attack on US buildings on US soil, many Americans retreated to a frontier mentality that showed itself in the form of cowboy masculinities and "mission accomplished" antics. At the same time, there was a general feeling that America had become "soft," that we needed to toughen up, say good-bye to feminism, and, basically, get back to traditional gender roles. As this toxic nationalist response faded slightly, a new message replaced it declaring that, far from the twenty-first century being the "end of feminism," it was instead the "end of men." While this seemed to constitute a feminist reaction to the 9/11 testosterone-fueled masculine nationalism, it was in fact arguing for the same thing from a new angle. So, if masculinist politics called for the end of feminism as a way of toughening up the nation and its defenses, pseudofeminists began to worry about whether we were too quick in dismissing "real men" and their masculinities, conjuring horror stories about what would happen if this new era really was "the end of men."

In 2010, the *Atlantic* featured as its cover story an article bluntly titled "The End of Men." The author, Hanna Rosin, reported on what she called an "unprecedented role reversal" within which women have become a majority in the workforce, in college, and in management positions. Rosin argued, in a clear and fairly compelling way, that postindustrial capitalism has been good to women in the workplace but fatal for male employment. And so, while men lose jobs and women keep theirs, while women pursue careers and men become househusbands, while women outnumber, outperform, and outlast men in higher education, Rosin sees a new gender order with women on top. Rather than finding some feminist optimism in these harbingers of change, however, Rosin sounds the alarm more often than not and seems to approve of predictions that the erosion of marriage may be good for women but that it will inevitably be disastrous for men and children. She also cites, somewhat approvingly, a by now hackneyed notion that women are setting their standards for men too high and that female disappointment in men is the real reason for the decline in marriages. She concludes her polemic by proposing that "the more women dominate, the more they behave, fittingly, like the dominant sex." This claim is backed up with a list of recent crimes, murders, and suicide bombings perpetrated by women. Rosin writes: "Rates of violence committed by middle-aged women have skyrocketed since the 1980s, and no one knows why. High-profile female killers have been showing up regularly in the news: Amy Bishop, the homicidal Alabama professor; Jihad Jane and her sidekick, Jihad Jamie; the latest generation of Black Widows, responsible for suicide bombings in Russia."[5]

There are so many conclusions that one could come to at the end of an article like Rosin's. Given that the new workplace seems to favor women over men and given that more and more women are in high-paid managerial positions, one could speculate on how corporate culture might change with women in charge. Or, given the statistics that she cites on the reorganization of the family, one might expect a kind of challenge to be issued to men to shape up or ship out. The essay really seems to be going in an altogether different direction until this last part. Like a romantic comedy that throws up every objection to the coupling of the male and female leads only to manufacture some farcical event that brings them back together again and makes them see the error of their ways, Rosin shows men and women moving in radically different directions and then concludes that maybe we need to opt again for traditional gender roles to right the sinking ship of marriage, family, and the social world built on the bedrock of heterosexuality. She comes up with one or two examples of violent women and concludes that women in charge are just as bad as men in charge.

Of course, I would not dispute the idea that women in charge may well be just as bad as their male equivalents, but this presumes that the *only* thing that has changed in the world of gender, labor, and social relations is the way that bodies are arranged within a gender hierarchy. In fact, the shifts that have created underemployment for men and a sense of the redundancy of maleness have also changed completely the structure of gender within which "male" and "female" once made sense.

Rosin adds a pop cultural spin to her argument at the end of her article by adding: "In her recent video, *Telephone*, Lady Gaga, with her infallible radar for the cultural edge, rewrites *Thelma and Louise* as a story not about elusive female empowerment but about sheer, ruthless power. Instead of killing themselves, she and her girlfriend (played by Beyoncé) kill a bad boyfriend and random others in a homicidal spree and then escape in their yellow pickup truck, Gaga bragging, 'We did it, Honey B.'"

While Rosin is calling our attention to the demise of an old-fashioned, anachronistic gender order, she is no gaga feminist. We'll pore over the subtle and not so subtle messages embedded in the Lady Gaga masterpiece *Telephone* later, but for now, suffice to say that Rosin's inability to parse the meaning of a contemporary pop video also hampers her ability to truly wrestle with the implications of the paradigm upon which she has stumbled. She's correct about a seismic shift under way on account of new gender roles in this new economy, but even as she acutely diagnoses the causes of these shifts, the categories of "men" and "women" remain remarkably stable and she fails to see that not only are gender roles crumbling but the very definitions of masculinity and femininity are under enormous pressure and have already mutated into new categories of difference. The *Atlantic* obviously got a lot of mileage out of its "End of Men" headline, which seemed to be tolling out the death knell on an era of gender relations. But ultimately neither the author nor the magazine, nor probably its readership, were all too interested in a real gender revolution.

Predictably, Rosin's polemic generated a number of responses in the blogosphere, mostly from people wanting to caution that the demise of men had been greatly exaggerated and that the upper echelons of corporate America has yet to show signs of a new gender order. Others saw Rosin's endism as a blatant attempt to fire up a debate where there was only enough material for a few comments about gender and the workplace. At the end of the day, Rosin named something real but she didn't go gaga on it; she didn't follow up on all the implications of the end of men. She also failed to make the necessary and inevitable connections to the rise of reproductive technologies that allow women to stretch out their reproductive years.

Another article in the same issue of the *Atlantic* by Pamela Paul did make the link to parenting, and asked a potentially even more provocative question: "Are Fathers Necessary?"[6] Given how many women parent alone (about 46 percent, says one CNN poll, of households in the United States are maintained by a single person, and 11.6 million single parents—mostly mothers—were living with their children in 2009), and given that men's contribution to family has been reduced in many cases to the role of sperm donor, this question is deeply relevant. While the "father knows best" model of functional parenting presumes that the sticky and sentimental matter of the maternal role must be offset by the hard and rational content of the paternal role, and given the endless conservative, and religious, warnings about what happens to children raised without fathers (they will turn out to be weak, gay, criminals, sexually confused, or all of the above), it has become hard to assess the actual relevancy of fatherhood. But in an age where more and more women parent alone rather than with a male partner, especially in African

American communities, and more children grow up with only
mediated relations to their deadbeat dads, the necessity of the
father falls into doubt.

As we saw earlier, black familial structures have been decimated by the long aftermath of slavery, and with so many black
and Latino men incarcerated (one in eleven black men, one in
twenty-seven Latinos, versus one in forty-five white men, according to 2011 findings from the US Bureau of Justice Statistics), many black households are without fathers for reasons
other than delinquency, disinterest, or extended adolescence.
The kinds of articles that feature journalists running through
the streets crying "the end of men" generally have white men in
mind, since if they were talking about men of color, this alarm-
ism would strike a very different chord. Given how many efforts
have been made in the United States and elsewhere to actually
eliminate black men, "the end of black men" would sound sinister rather than prophetic, descriptive rather than predictive, and
would easily feed into eugenicist fantasies of socially engineered
white domination.

As the stock of white masculinity goes into some kind of
slow decline, as fatherhood fades and the family morphs into an
amalgam of invested adults and dependent children, we should
prepare ourselves to reckon with the form, the content, and the
meanings of new household formations for varied communities.
Indeed, in this shifting landscape of white male redundancy, the
news of a pregnant man should have been received as a little
ray of hope for male reproductive futurity and as a sign that
masculinity had a place in the new domestic order after all. Of
course, the pregnant man, in the end, is a storm in a turkey
baster, just a part of a sea change in reproductive politics, one
that has produced a rise in the medical industry of assisted fertility for wealthy couples who choose to have kids later in life; a

boom in lesbian and gay childrearing; and a seismic shift in the meaning of "family" and "parent."

MODERN FAMILIES

So how have Americans explained these new domestic arrangements to themselves? What new narratives have popped up in the media to contend with the reorganized family? Predictably, the "new" narratives tend to sneak the old family in the back door of the new family's house. Witness the strange phenomenon of a very popular TV series that premiered in 2006 on HBO, authored by two gay men and telling the story of an alternative family who had to hide from their neighbors and friends and pretend to be normal while living a complex and different reality behind closed doors. Was this newly popular alternative family gay? Lesbian? Transgendered? Made up of multiple immigrant families sharing resources? Was it an extended black family reinventing kinship? No, the show in question, *Big Love,* represented a Mormon family committed to polygamous or multiple marriage and featured a husband, three wives, and many children. American viewers were indeed challenged to confront the reality of diverse household forms, but the series gambled on the idea that Americans prefer their modern families to come dressed in the same religious vestments as their old families. *Big Love* offers a deeply patriarchal and conservative family as salvation for the institutions of marriage and kinship in a time of multiple crises in the domestic realm.

In fact, it turns out that American audiences can more easily accommodate narratives of Mormon polygamy than they can conceive (pun intended) of a continuum of artificial-reproduction narratives that include pregnant men and lesbian mums. *Big Love* features at its center a polygamous family consisting of a man, Bill Henrickson (Bill Paxton), and his three wives (Barb,

played by Jeanne Tripplehorn; Nicki, played by Chloe Sevigny;
and Margie, played by Ginnifer Goodwin) and their children.
Having broken away from a polygamous cult in Juniper Creek,
Utah, Bill lives under cover in Sandy, Utah, and opens up some
home-improvement stores while struggling to balance business,
his secret life, and the needs and desires of three wives. Drama
develops between Bill and his father-in-law Roman (Nicki's father), the Juniper Creek cult leader and "prophet," between Bill's
mother and father, between and among the wives, and between
Bill and the people with whom he works. The unusual family
struggles to preserve their way of life by keeping out of the public eye and dodging accusations of perversion while thinking of
themselves as the apex of traditional family values.

Despite an ongoing discourse about the diversity of polygamous marriage in the series, within which the sister-wives understand themselves as married as much to each other as they are
to Bill, the intimacy never crosses from the emotional into the
physical. While most polygamous structures (harem, purdah,
zenena) are also thought to be sanctuaries of unspoken female-
female eroticism, *Big Love*, despite being the brainchild of gay
couple Mark V. Olsen and Will Scheffer, barely touches on the
potential for lesbianism within plural marriage and also side-
steps the questions of whether polygamous households might be
abusive to women. When asked about this in an interview, Olsen
said: "Some feminists argued back in the '60s and '70s that marriage was inherently abusive and patriarchal—that it was not a
good deal for women. As the feminist movement has matured,
there has been an evolution in that thinking. Polygamy can grow
into a healthier model for some women."[7] Apart from the deeply
problematic notion of an immature version of feminism that had
a problem with marriage but came to see the error of its ways
(!!), this answer reveals one of the most galling premises of the

show—namely that polygamy (i.e., one man with many wives, not all partners taking multiple partners) is perfectly acceptable, that it is analogous to other minority sexual practices (like S/M or homosexuality), and that people should recognize the spiritual depth that fuels the practice and ignore the child brides, the brainwashing of children, and the patriarchal premises of a system that assigns multiple wives to individual men.

The show is complex in many ways, and in later seasons it grappled with the questions of female autonomy and male homosexuality directly, but, like so much of the popular culture created in the past twenty years or so by gay men (*Desperate Housewives*, for example, and *Golden Girls*, both penned by Marc Cherry), *Big Love* concerns itself with a very broad and general model of sexual liberation but doesn't worry about whether gender liberation is part of the package. And again, despite these shows centering upon female bonding (and fighting) in a majority-female household, lesbianism is the love that dare not speak its name.

As we saw with the artificial-reproduction films, Hollywood's take on new and diverse household forms still privileges the nuclear triangle of mommy, daddy, and baby makes three over all other forms of alliance and relation. In *The Switch*, Jennifer Aniston's character had to anxiously make it clear that her choice to reproduce without a boyfriend or husband did not mean she was a lesbian. And her ability to get pregnant on the very first try implied a kind of love-at-first-sight version of reproductive capability—in other words, her egg and her best friend's sperm were fated to be together, and her immediate pregnancy was proof of their compatibility.

So what happens when we try to tell stories about alternative families, lesbian moms, for example? Do we find alternative narratives about reproduction, family, and love *there*?

Apparently, 2010 was a very good year for artificial-insemination films. Lisa Cholodenko, a lesbian, directed a film that focused upon the lesbian parenting boom. *The Kids Are All Right* represented the not-so-pretty sight of lesbian overparenting in the form of the double jeopardy of the two-mom family, and it, unwittingly perhaps, made the argument that equal opportunity means equal chance to fuck up your kids and extend the tyranny of the nuclear family. In fact, *The Kids Are All Right* is a soul-crushing depiction of long-term relationships, lesbian parenting, and midlife crisis.

In the film, Nic (Annette Bening) and Jules (Julianne Moore) are mushed into one category by their kids, Laser (Josh Hutcherson) and Joni (Mia Wasikowska), who call them "moms" or "the moms." The moms have merged into one maternal entity, and although they have distinct personalities, their parenting function is depicted as one amorphous smothering gesture after another. The kids suffer through, but crisis ensues when Laser decides to track down his sperm-donor dad, Paul (Mark Ruffalo). Once Paul rides onto the scene on his classic black BMW motorcycle, bearing organic veggies and good wine, cracks in the façade of lesbian domesticity appear and a rather predictable cycle of betrayal, infidelity, and domestic upheaval begins.

While Cholodenko's first film, the 1998 *High Art*, played against stereotype by setting its lesbian drama in a drugged-out contemporary art world, *The Kids Are All Right* loads sexual inertia, domestic dowdiness, and bourgeois complacency onto the lesbian couple and leaves the sperm-donor dad in the enviable position of being free, cool, and casually sexual. Early on in the film, Jules and Nic watch gay porn while making a grand effort to have sex. In this cringe-worthy scene, Jules goes under the covers to go down on Nic, who keeps watching the porn with no particular desire. Eventually we hear the whirr of a vibrator, but still there is no money shot (either in the bed or on the TV screen), no real desire between the two women, and not even any flesh! Cut to Paul making love to a gorgeous African American woman, one of his employees, no less, with much gusto, much nakedness, and free abandon. OK, we get the picture, long-term relationships struggle with desire, short-term involvements struggle with commitment. The long-term couple may not have great sex but they do have the family and togetherness, the single guy has great sex and lots of it but no one to go home to.

While the film's moral outcome is designed to favor the women and leave Paul out in the cold, it actually delivers, whether the film means to or not, a scathing critique of gay marriage. If the message here is "see, gay marriages are just like straight ones—we all face the same problems," then surely the outcome of the film would be the end of marriage, the desire to find other kinds of arrangements that work—gaga feminism, anyone? But no, this film, like many a heterosexual drama that turns the family inside out only to return to it at the end, shows that marriage is sexless, families turn rotten with familiarity, lesbians are flawed parents—and then ultimately asks us to invest hope in this very arrangement.

The Kids Are All Right is beautifully acted and has moments when it gets everything right—the awkwardness between Paul and Joni and Laser, for example, at their first meeting; the anger sparked by Paul trying to step in and offer parenting advice to Nic (she responds: "I need your advice like I need a dick up my butt!"—possibly the best line in the film), the irritation between Nic and Jules as they try to absorb the daddy-come-lately into their family unit. But all this great acting cannot save a conservative script from its own conclusions. Even though the film is quite good at showing how superfluous and redundant the father role has become in an era of the supermom, by refusing

to distinguish between the "moms" and by not making much
of a gender distinction between Nic (vaguely butch) and Jules
(vaguely femme), we are left with too much mothering and a
sense that fatherhood is necessary to intervene in the cloying
attentions of maternal love. In one stinging exchange, Laser is
leaving for the evening and both moms reach out their arms to
him asking for hugs. Laser says to Nic—"Hug *her*"—meaning
Jules—"that's what she's there for!" It is a laugh line for sure but
it somehow seals the moms in asexual pathos and interferes with
our ability to really identify with them.

There are parts of the movie that fuel the disdain that the
audience might begin to feel for the moms. We are not given
enough info about the basis for their original love and attraction;
a quick story about how they met refers to flirtatious attraction
between the two, but this sexual energy is told rather than depicted. At the same time, Paul's effect on women is depicted but
not told—he does not charm or romance women; with seemingly no action on his part, women simply throw themselves at
him. This naturalization of his sexual power and the naturalization of the lack of charisma of the moms again stabilizes a
grid of desire that always tips in favor of male heterosexuality
and leaves lesbians stranded. With the scales tipped this way, it
becomes inevitable that Jules will sleep with Paul, that Nic will
be cast as the sad, slightly butch partner who loses out to the
dynamic, phallic dad. Again, this could have been played differently—Nic could have been overtly butch; she would have
been much more likely in fact to ride the BMW motorbike than
Paul (classic Beemers are a popular queer choice of motorcycle);
she could have been phallic with a dildo instead of flaccid with
a vibrator. I'm not advocating that the lesbian relationship be
positive and male heterosexuality be slammed—but I am arguing that Cholodenko is working the well-worn grooves of the

cinematic depiction of lesbian desire as a flickering flame always on the verge of extinction and of lesbian-male rivalry as always a mismatch.

Finally, if *The Kids Are All Right* wanted to weigh in on the gay-marriage debate by saying that marriage sucks anyway and here's a realistic depiction of what long-term relationships look like, I could live with that. If the film wanted to take a hard look at lesbian parenting and refute the idea that too many moms spoil the broth, I would have embraced that. If it wanted to offer a critique of fatherhood as always too little, too late, I would have applauded that. But to give us cloying lesbian moms, charismatic fathers, inert long-term relationships, and then to tell us to accept it, get used to it, and like it or lump it . . . well, why?

If I learned anything from Cholodenko's film, it is that trading in sex for comfort, change for stability, and improvised relationships for marriage are all bad deals, and if we don't change the social structures we inherit, we are doomed to repeat them.

THE LAW OF THE BUTCH FATHER

What *The Kids Are All Right* left out, and what the incident of the pregnant man bypassed in the sensation around his transgender embodiment, was the quiet revolution in parenting that may have been affected by the phenomenon of the *butch dad*— the lesbian parent, in other words, who is variantly gendered and therefore not a mother but not recognized socially as a father. While the pregnant man got all the press, and while lesbian moms get all the respect, butch-femme partners may well be the place to look for real shifts in the logic of parenting. I'm not saying simply that the straight world of parenting can more easily manage to incorporate the trans-man dad than the butch dad, or that progressive hetero parents can easily acclimate to the seemingly bonus package of two moms while they may cringe at the butch-femme couple, but I am saying that the assault on fatherhood launched by the butch is very possibly the untold story of this reproductive revolution. And it is the butch father that heralds a gaga feminist component to the new queer family in his/her ability to break in on the fortress of fatherhood that has been preserved for men and men only.

Some queer theorists have grappled with the question of whether the father role has to be occupied by a male-bodied person; others have thought through the dynamics of double motherhood; but most queer theorists, like everyone else, seem to want to assign parenting roles by sex, and thus the whole family grid seems oddly stable. The butch dad and the femme mom raise the possibility of authority without patriarchy (because the butch does not access male privilege), gender polarity without compulsory heterosexuality (because the femme does not always access heterosexual privilege), and they make possible an education for potentially gender-normative kids in the arbitrariness of all gender roles—so kids raised by a femme mother and a butch father might learn about gendered forms of power untethered to gender hierarchies; they might see masculinity and femininity as more malleable, and they might understand gender as something that someone does rather than something that someone is: kids find terms for gender-variant adults—boygirl, inbetweeners—and they come up with multiple explanations for gender variance, explanations, moreover, that adults lack, and so we can learn from kids being raised by butch-femme couples about how to live in a contingent relation to gender and gender norms.

Queer parenting duos, to the extent that they do not neatly fall into the gay daddies or lesbian moms categories, also offer straight couples more options for how to do their gender dynamics. While parenting dynamics fall into seemingly organic grooves, his and her modes of dividing labor and responsibilities, those divisions might be suddenly illuminated and take on the glow of absurdity when a queer couple is present. For example, when my partner and I attended a parents' meeting organized informally in relation to our kids' school, we were a bit bewildered by the ways the hetero couples divided their domains and authority. When it came time to cease socializing for a while and discuss some issues at the school, the parents formed two concentric circles. The inner circle was made up exclusively of women, who were sitting and already involved in animated conversations about the school, their kids, and education in general. The outer circle consisted of men, and they stood up (the better to slip out unnoticed?) and chatted distractedly with a buddy or remained silent. It was confusing. Where should I sit/stand? The room finally quieted down and we went around to do introductions. Remarkably, only the women introduced themselves, saying who they were, the status of their child in the school, and the kinds of concerns they brought to the meeting. The men did not introduce themselves, nor were they asked to do so. Finally, when it was my turn to say something, I introduced myself and then said that I would like to hear from the men. This caused a ripple of surprise, but then the guys did begin to introduce themselves, one by one giving their names and then offering an account of the kind of support they offered their wives and partners, whose job it was to figure out the immensely complicated questions concerning schooling, play dates, extracurricular activity, and so on. By the end of the meeting, the inner circle had closed its ranks and was engaged in the hard work of educational activism, the outer circle had wandered off to check on the kids, drink coffee, and chat on the balcony.

The meeting was a fascinating illustration of the ways in which men and women unconsciously divide the world up into masculine and feminine realms of action and activity. The division is by no means equitable, fair, or even logical, but apparently it seems that way to the men and women who fall easily into these intuitive and unquestioned divisions of labor and spheres of influence. Indeed, as many sociologists have empirically shown—and really there are endless studies on the persistence of a gender split in domestic labor—the realms of responsibility that fall to women tend to be much more extensive and onerous when it comes to domestic labor, material and immaterial, than those that fall to men. However, weirdly, women and men feel as if they have made a very reasonable, fair division of time and labor, and so when researchers ask husbands and wives what kind of division of labor takes place in their households, both partners tend to reply "fifty-fifty," when in fact the division is much more often an eighty-twenty or seventy-thirty split. This phenomenon, of shifting modes of gendered labor that go unaccompanied by changes in domestic labor divisions, has been well-recognized, and gave rise to the term "the second shift" or "the double shift," after Arlie Hochschild's groundbreaking book of 1989.[8] In her book, Hochschild pointed out to readers that despite the many inroads that feminism had made, gendered divisions of labor remained constant. And she asked: "If more mothers of small children are stepping into full-time jobs outside the home, and if most couples can't afford household help, how much more are fathers doing at home?" The answer, predictably, was "not much!" What's more, even back in 1989, more than 20 years ago, researchers like Hochschild were asking what this unequal division of labor "does for love and marriage in an age of high divorce."[9] While a straightforward feminist reading of this phenomenon would use the unequal division of labor and women's misrecognition of their own contributions as evidence of the way that women's subordination is accomplished materially *and* ideologically, a gaga feminist would claim that while divisions of labor do not need to be fifty-fifty or even sixty-forty, they do need to be acknowledged and chosen. In other words, people can make whatever decisions they choose about who does what in the home; some women will cook more, some men may do more laundry, some feminine partners may want to be more career oriented, some masculine partners may want to spend more time with children. But like all aspects of a partnership, roles must be negotiated, sorted through, agreed upon rather than divided according to some divine, mysterious, and increasingly impractical plan.

So let's break it down: in a world where women are doing 80 percent of the work for only 50 percent of the credit, in a society where many fortysomething men leave their wives for younger versions of them, at a time when sex scandals involving older men in very public offices (Dominique Strauss-Kahn, Arnold Schwarzenegger) are in abundance, surely some heterosexual middle-aged women want other options. And of course, there actually are other options. But compulsory heterosexuality is a system that makes it seem as if heterosexuality, with all of its imperfections and flaws and glitches, is the only game in town. What if there were other games, as compelling and potentially more equitable and easily as sexy as the heterosexual game?

BEYONCÉ ON THE PHONE FOR GAGA

And finally, for now, what do Lady Gaga and Beyoncé have to say about living in a "man's world" while reinventing womanhood? While some feminists like Camille Paglia, Susan Faludi, and Hanna Rosin have found Lady Gaga's video *Telephone* to be no big deal and maybe even regressive, we might look to its landscape for a more upbeat, wacky, and anarchist take on "the end of men."

In *Telephone*, Lady Gaga and Beyoncé trip and bounce through a pop anthem about women, desire, and the end of men—the scene is set in a women's prison and does not shy away from "negative images" of queers: butch prison guards and tranny inmates abound, for example. (This is not a comment on actual prisons so much as on the prison of representation itself and the formulaic sign systems we use to represent otherness.) The song itself, misleadingly pop in tone, is actually about broken communications, phones that ring but don't get answered, messages that never get picked up, missed connections, texts that are never sent, words that are never spoken. The opening drawn-out scene shows Lady Gaga prowling for action, climbing the walls of the women's jail and sparking fights in the mess hall. It also serves as the prelude for a killing spree, and it ties Gaga and Beyoncé to a kind of Valerie Solanas (the wild feminist from the 1970s who shot Andy Warhol and wrote the *SCUM Manifesto* arguing for the "cutting up [of] men") version of feminism, a dark feminism, a Thelma and Louise ride against domestic violence, the law, patriarchy. It is also a feminism built around stutter steps, hesitation, knowing and unknowing, embracing your darkness. It is an anti-marriage, pro-promiscuity feminism, one that does not find comfort in assimilation but demands resistance and transformation.

While the easy gloss on the gendered meaning of "telephone" would cast woman as the silent receiver, patiently waiting for a call, and would picture the man as the active gentleman caller deciding when and where to push the buttons, in actual fact the song and the video refuse this gender scheme. The ear and the phone are neither vagina and penis nor speaker and listener; in this agenda-bending extravaganza, the telephone is a philosopher's wet dream, a vessel that allows us to theorize connection itself. And, by the way, what's up with divas and phones? Remember that Blondie was hanging on one, Madonna was hanging one up, even Beyoncé, in "If I Was a Boy," was turning one off and telling everyone her phone was down to give herself cover for infidelities. Avital Ronell, a philosopher of technology and knowledge, and gaga in her own way, wrote *The Telephone Book* in 1989 about the invention of the telephone, the new forms of self that this technology (as revolutionary in its time as the Internet) enabled, and the kind of calls that actually go out, ideologically speaking, between people and culture. "It is a question of answerability," says Ronell. "You picking it up means the call has come through."[10]

The blogosphere is full of critical readings and revelations about Lady Gaga's *Telephone*—it is a Foucauldian take on prison and "technological entrapment"; Tavia Nyong'o read it as the channeling of Judith Butler's cult essay "The Lesbian Phallus"; it is obscene, murderous, cruel to animals, misogynist, man-hating, homophobic, and heterophobic; and I think you could safely place it as a Deleuzian exploration of flow and affect, not to mention an episode in object-oriented philosophy.

While *Telephone* ostensibly stretches a mindless pop song about a missed phone call into a wild ride through American popular culture, Lady Gaga manages to harness her ring tones to much deeper concepts, like the fragmentation of connection in the age of cell phones, the creation of new forms of rebellion in a universe of media manipulation, and the emergence of new forms of gender and sexuality in a digital age. The video, which accompanied the song of the same name, went viral soon after appearing on the Internet, and by some estimates, it racked up a few million viewers overnight. *Telephone* mixes interesting visual landscapes—color saturated, shiny like candy and bursting with Americana—with innovative soundscapes full of stutters and clicks. Add a few outrageous costumes, a story about two

ladies on the run and engaged in homicidal ventures, moving
across the screen in a "pussy wagon" right out of the film *Kill
Bill*, and overnight you have a pop phenomenon.

So what is the "telephone" in this sonic drama and what is
Gaga doing with it? Many of the phones in the film are land-
lines—the phone in the jail (or "club" as Gaga calls it), the green
phone in Beyoncé's bedroom, the blue phone that Lady Gaga
wears as she makes sandwiches—these phones are fixed in place,
not mobile, wearable but also restricting. The push and pull of
the game of telephone as it plays out in the video resembles the
rhythms of hetero dating: she waits, he calls; she answers, he
speaks; she yells, he hangs up. But the telephone imagery also
refers to stalking—the phrase that repeats in the Gaga song is
"stop calling, stop calling." The mobile phone is a player in
the battle of lovers, and so Lady Gaga and Beyoncé decide to
unleash themselves from the tyranny of the phone—instead of
hanging on the telephone, they become the telephone. The music
pulses like a ring tone (like the ring tone it is about to anyway
become); it burbles and beeps, hiccups and repeats, insistently,
calling and ringing, ringing and calling and chaining us all to
the charisma of the pop beat even as heterosexuality itself seems
like an event in a distant past. The video makes violence against
men into its signature and its enigma and it asks, obliquely,
what comes next?

THREE

Gaga Sexualities:
The End of Normal

*Mrs. Fox: We are all different. But especially him
[indicating Mr. Fox]. But there's something fantastic
about that, isn't there?*

—Wes Anderson's *Fantastic Mr. Fox*

NEW BALLS PLEASE!

A couple of years ago, our neighbor asked my girlfriend and me
if she could feature us in an article she was writing about women
who leave their male partners and then date other women. We
had a couple of problems with that formulation: first, my girlfriend was already separated from her husband when we started
dating; second, I don't identify in any simple way as a "woman";
and lastly, well, the whole article seemed to want to leave heterosexuality intact as a kind of natural framework into which you
insert the butch in place of the bio man and everything proceeds
as usual. This was a recipe for disaster, and indeed, the resulting
O Magazine article has haunted us ever since with its simplistic
accounts of newly single straight women who, looking for partners to help them raise their kids, tumble into bed with other
women.[1] The article made the formerly straight women sound
like intrepid explorers in the borderlands of gender and sexuality
who wander off the straight and narrow path of heterosexuality
only to stumble upon a strange tribe of butches. The butches are

depicted not as attractive or sexy in their own right but rather as
expedient, useful, good companions and providers.

There was a smidgeon of truth in this depiction, but generally
speaking the article could not imagine the actual impetus for formerly heterosexual women to move from men to "pseudomen,"
and so the whole thing sounded like a massive compromise for
the women, perpetuating the depiction of butches as always a
last resort rather than a deliberate choice. In fact, the system in
which girls and boys come to understand sexual mores makes it
impossible for any woman to even think about choosing butches
as their masculine partners, since butch masculinity is always
represented as an abject and gross perversion of "the real thing."

However, as I explored in another book, *The Queer Art of
Failure*, there are actually many representations available to children within which very queer arrangements present themselves
as viable alternatives to naturalized heterosexuality. Take, for
example, one of my all-time favorite films: *Finding Nemo*. *Finding Nemo*, in its own queerly aquatic way, represents a scenario
in which a family (in this case, a family of clownfish) has to reor-
ganize itself quickly and effectively after the loss of the mother.
When Nemo's family is attacked by a barracuda in the film's
grim opening minutes, Nemo and his neurotic father, Marlin,
have to rethink their meaning, their relations to one another and
to the larger oceanic community, and they each learn to swim
along different currents precisely by getting lost, wandering
away from the tried and the true and finding new forms of life.
Enter Dory, the forgetful queer fish voiced by Ellen DeGeneres.
While Dory may not have much of a memory, in her queerly
butch way, she knows lots of stuff—she reads, speaks whale,
can follow the ocean tides to Australia—and in the process of
helping Marlin find the abducted Nemo, Dory manages to ar-
ticulate a different mode of being female (she is not a mother),

a different mode of parenting (she has no memory so cannot draw upon a vast repertoire of parenting techniques), a different form of romance (she has no interest in Marlin). Dory is a butch fish, and her eclectic mode of being encourages everyone around her to rearticulate his or her own sense of connections. I am not saying that *Finding Nemo* deliberately presents child viewers with a gay scenario disguised as a fish cartoon; rather, I am trying to show that once you stray from representational modes dependent upon human forms and all the cliché-ridden formulae that they entail, surprisingly new narratives of life, love, and intimacy are bound to appear. That these narratives do appear in animated films for children comes as no surprise.[2]

So, with all of these analogies to fish, the life aquatic, and oceanic movements in hand, let's go back to the drawing board and track what's happening with straight women at the same time that trans men are getting pregnant and dykes are becoming daddies.

New affiliations between bodies, sex, and power remind us that the categories of being that seemed to specify and define human nature over one hundred years ago have quickly become rather inadequate placeholders for identity. While "male" and "female" are categories crumbling under the weight of revision, institutions like marriage are similarly taking on water and slowly sinking into the morass of spoiled intimacies and forced nuclearity—fewer people are married by their late twenties than ever before in history. Rather than fixing these categories and institutions, feminist and queer theory should be giving them a good shove into the muck. However, out in the mainstream marketplace of ideas, a place badly in need of old-fashioned as well as newfangled feminisms, best-selling books are still telling straight women how to get men and how to marry them, and telling men how and why they should become properly domesticated.

From Lori Gottlieb's desperation in the 2010 best-selling
Marry Him, to apocalyptic pronouncements in the news about
gender imbalances in college; from romantic comedies in which
women throw themselves at men, begging to get married, to romantic comedies in which men barricade themselves in garages
with other men to get away from women (*I Love You, Man; He's
Just Not That Into You; Bride Wars; The Hangover,* all made
in 2009), signs of trouble are brewing in white heterosexuality.
Gottlieb, a graduate of the "beggars can't be choosers" school of
feminism, thinks the problem is that the average white straight
woman has impossibly high standards and that no man can ever
live up to the ideals of romance to which she clings. While it is
OK to have high standards in your twenties and thirties, Gottlieb warns, by your forties, when men are thin on the ground
and biological clocks are ticking, you better grab a partner, any
partner (short, balding, with physically repulsive mannerisms or
socially inexcusable hobbies), and—yup, you guessed it—marry
him! One might be forgiven for thinking that if straight women's
standards go any lower, they may as well see eligibility in a male
blow-up doll. And really, "the eligible man" is already a highly
flexible category that manages to incorporate everything from
the six-foot-something sporty smart guy with a sense of humor
and a little cash to the twitchy video geek with body odor. Indeed, the Judd Apatow machine (*Knocked Up; Forgetting Sarah
Marshall; Superbad*) has made the nerd and his dweeb friends
into bastions of sexy new masculinities.

Gottlieb blames feminism for the epidemic of single women,
saying that young women who believed in feminism basically
"empowered ourselves out of a good mate."[3] A good mate here
is basically any man who will marry you, and no other option
will do—not a female-bodied male, a transgender man, a life of
dating and good friends, singledom—nothing but marriage. The

marriage mania, an obsession instilled in young women along with the color pink around age three, is never the problem for Gottlieb, only the inability to find a good man. But as academic Lauren Berlant writes, "The female complaint is a discourse of disappointment . . . where love is concerned, disappointment is a partner to fulfillment, not an opposite."[4]

So what's a girl to do? Can women reconcile to disappointment and loss and learn to live differently? At least one answer comes in the form of the straight woman who becomes interested in butches or trans men. For the heterosexually inclined, nonhomophobic woman who is not totally averse to silicone dicks, the butch/trans masculinity option can look pretty good at that time of life that we cruelly call middle-age, when straight men hook up with very young women and straight women find that their dating options are among the retirement crowd. If straight men average about three marriages over the course of a lifetime, then the odds are not good for the straight woman in her forties or fifties looking to meet someone her own age. While for Gottlieb, the fortysomething-year-old woman without a man has no one to blame but herself, the musical-chairs model of heterosexual dating always leaves someone without a place at the table. This alone cannot explain the rise in middle-aged, later-life coming-out stories for feminine women, and on its own this would be a rather homophobic explanation anyway, but the imbalances between male and female dating options certainly open the door to, shall we say, the appeal of alternative lifestyles.

There is some historical evidence that divorced women have often combined their households to get by, but most historians are loath to attribute any sexual motives to these unions. Nowadays, however, new attention is being paid, by scientists, no less, to "heteroflexible" desires or to the phenomenon of heterosexual women whose desire for masculinity or masculine bodies can wander (the literal meaning of "perversion") to female-bodied or trans-bodied people. An article in the *New York Times Magazine* from 2009 by Daniel Bergner titled "What Do Women Want?"[5] cited studies by Meredith Chivers and others on gendered sexual response and reported that the studies showed that while heterosexual men respond quickly and obviously to images of women, heterosexual and lesbian, they respond hardly at all to gay pornography of sexy images of men. And gay men respond definitively to sexy images of the male body, but not at all to images of female bodies. But women, straight and lesbian, respond equally to images of men and women, although their level of arousal depends on situations rather than the body itself. The article noted that women, lesbians and heterosexuals, revealed a mismatch between body and mind when their degrees of physical arousal and their reports about their arousal did not match up. Indeed, Bergner writes: "No matter what their self-proclaimed sexual orientation, they showed, on the whole, strong and swift genital arousal when the screen offered men with men, women with women and women with men. They responded objectively much more to [an image of an] exercising woman than to [a] strolling man, and their blood flow rose quickly—and markedly, though to a lesser degree than during all the human scenes except the footage of the ambling, strapping man—as they watched the apes [images of animals having sex in Discovery-channel-type type shows]. And with the women, especially the straight women, mind and genitals seemed scarcely to belong to the same person."

Bergner, the author of a book on fetishistic desires titled *The Other Side of Desire*, like so many other authors surveyed in this book, sees "woman" and "man" as remarkably consistent categories; for him, the question "What do women want?" makes sense because "women" as a group are a stable and known category. But the basic assumption of much queer theory, an assumption that often does not travel far beyond the university, is that both "men" and "women" are culturally constructed categories, as are the terms "masculinity" and "femininity," and that there is no essential set of traits, desires, or inclinations that defines men in opposition to women and vice versa. It is unfortunate that the theoretical undoing of gender stability has had so little impact out in the real world. It's too bad, in other words, that people still think of men and women as if they are alien species from Mars and Venus, respectively, and that they cannot see the multiple differences that disaggregate each category and that prevent large-scale pronouncements about what "women" like or how "men" behave or why "women like chocolate" and "men love football." If we could actually see these gender categories as saturated with contradictions, as discontinuous across all the bodies they are supposed to describe, then we could begin to notice the odd forms of gender, the gaga genders, that have multiplied like computer viruses in late capitalist cultures.

Much of what we call heterosexuality, in fact, as Bergner's work on fetishism itself demonstrates, has little to do with normative pathways of desire and sexual practice. Some heterosexualities use the "beard" of marriage to cover over some truly outrageous and wild desires. Let me give one example that I stumbled across of a seemingly normative arrangement that was undoubtedly intensified and underwritten by some decidedly nonnormative practices. I was traveling to Indiana to give a talk, and my flight arrived very late at night in Indianapolis, where I was to be picked up and driven by limo to Bloomington. The pickup went flawlessly, and soon I was sitting in the back of a limousine, zooming along an empty freeway in the middle of Indiana. The driver and I started a casual conversation—How was he? What did he do when he wasn't driving? How did he

like living in Indiana? The driver told me he had lived in the state
his whole life but only recently moved from one small town to
another. He had relocated after a divorce from his wife, with
whom he had run a small business. What kind of business? I
inquired . . . maybe I shouldn't have. "We hand-bred horses,"
he replied. Well, I am a city person, urban through and through,
and this rang no bells for me. "Hand-bred?" I mused, almost
to myself. All that came to mind was an episode from the second season of the MTV show *Jackass*, where the professional
morons are inseminating a cow by hand using a turkey baster
or something. So I pursued it a bit further. "Do you mean you
had to artificially inseminate the horses?" No, no, he replied. It
wasn't artificial. Hmm. Odd then, how did the "hand-breeding"
enter in? I wondered aloud. My informant responded, in a completely even tone, as if we were discussing his being a salesman
at Target, "Well, sometimes when you want the horses to mate,
you have to help the male get in the female." This really stumped
me. "Doesn't the stud know how to get into the mare?" I asked,
proud of myself for using the horse terms for male and female.
"You'd be surprised, miss," came the answer. I *was* surprised!
(Miss? Really?) Why would a male horse need help entering a
female horse—isn't that stuff just, I don't know, natural? The
answer took me even more by surprise: "More often than not,
the stud finds the anus and does his business there."

Anus. There it was, a word I had not expected or wanted
to hear on a dark night's ride in Indiana. It got weirder. OK, I
allowed, so the stud needs help finding the right place to enter
the mare, but again, where does the "hand-breeding" bit come
in to this scenario? "Well, miss," (puh-leeze!), the driver continued, "basically, while my wife held the mare at one end, I
would have to guide the stud into the mare's vagina at the other
end." Wow, really? People do this? "That sounds, um, danger-

ous," I said blankly. "Oh, it is dangerous, all right," my friend answered. "On some days, that stud was like a raging rapist." Again, not words you want to hear out in the middle of nowhere after midnight from a stranger. "Oh yeah?" I said. "Yes, and truly, miss, you cannot imagine what it feels like to have three hundred pounds of raging cock in your hands." True, I could not imagine, I did not want to imagine. Weird! "So, let me get this right," I ventured. "You had to literally hold the horse's penis and guide him into the mare while your wife held the mare still." "Yes ma'am." So, I wondered, what happened, after this little ritual? Did it influence their sex life? Stimulate it? Destroy it? I didn't ask these questions, obviously, and the driver only underscored that the work was very dangerous; it once got out of hand, so to speak, when a stud tore down the stable. Not surprisingly, his wife didn't want to continue the work, and soon after this incident, they divorced. There was so much in this story that intrigued me, and I thought about it throughout my visit to Bloomington. When I relayed the episode to a colleague she accused me of being patronizing toward people who live in small-town America.

But was that it, really? Was this merely a case of an urban queer person puzzling over the odd ways of country folk? Or was this story a reminder, in fact, that human lives and their stories are intricately woven through and into nonhuman animal lives and stories? And that what seems natural in humans and nonhuman animals is totally a fantasy, when we come down to it? This story, like many others I could tell or that you yourself might think of, confirms in many ways that the concept of "normal" has reached a kind of conceptual conclusion.

Heterosexuality, this kind of story shows, is rife with external influences, some coming from the context within which the relationship occurs, some from the individuals' biographies, some from animal worlds, and so on and so forth. There really is little in the way of a normal core to any set of sexualities; "normal" is just the name we give to the cleaned-up versions of sex that we wish to endorse on behalf of social stability and moral order. In reality, sex is both much more wild than our norms allow for and, at times, much more bland and banal than our concerns for moral order indicate.

HOW GLOBAL IS GAY?

While I found, on my trip to Indiana, that there is an extraordinary range to the meaning of heterosexuality in North America by region, by class, certainly by race (what are the connections between rural whiteness and beastiality, for example?), when we look at the ways that the US models of sex and gender get imported around the globe, we might be surprised to see how compact and simple, obvious and inevitable these classification systems can look. Even though homosexuality means one thing to a white gay man living in rural Indiana, another to an urban Latino in New York, and something else entirely to an Asian American lesbian in San Francisco, there exists a so-called global gay template for both sexual identity and social tolerance of sexual minorities, and these tend to be modeled on a fictitious but powerful fantasy of the United States. In this fantasy, gays and lesbians and trans people enjoy complete acceptance and live happily in same-sex relationships accepted by their parents and coworkers alike. This same fantasy compels people who feel persecuted elsewhere by restrictive models of sexual conformity to think of the United States as a sanctuary. It also has the unfortunate effect of homogenizing sexual systems around the world through the work of nongovernmental organizations and various other outreach groups.

In fact, as gender/sex systems become ever more complicated and unstable in Euro-American cultures shaken by precipitous declines in marriage rates and rocketing increases in divorces, altered from within by new gender systems and emergent sexual vernaculars, it is perhaps *only* the global circulation of Euro-American sex/gender systems that lends them any stability at all. What is wobbly and precarious at home looks sturdy and lasting when imported elsewhere; and so, as folks furiously debate gay marriage, gays in the military, and gay labor issues in the United States, "global gay" discourses transform contested categories and uneven political fields into stable identities and a politics of inclusion/exclusion. This often has the effect of imposing regulations onto pleasurably chaotic domains of behavior (cruising among men who may not identify as gay, for example) and substituting streamlined identity formations (gay, lesbian, transgendered) for extremely complex local organizations of bodies, desires, sex, and kinship, many of which are stratified less by sexual orientation than by, say, labor or age.

Let me give some examples. Some categories of gender variance, for example, in eastern Europe, the Middle East, and India and China allow for female children to be raised as boys where a family farm requires male rather than female labor, or where boys are so prized that a family with only daughters is at a distinct disadvantage. The *New York Times*, for example, in 2010 ran a story about girls whose parents dressed them as boys in Afghanistan. So elaborate was this phenomenon that there is even a name for such children in Dari: *bacha posh*. The girls who occupy this category enjoy greater mobility than their sisters and might access education more easily too.[6] Inevitably, however, they are forced back into womanhood when they become marriageable, and for many, this is a shock and a rough transition.

In other countries, Albania, for example, girls raised as boys continue to live as men when they reach adulthood and are allowed to take wives. Two years before they ran the story on *ba-cha posh* in Afghanistan, the *New York Times* presented another story of female gender shifting: under the headline "Sworn to Virginity and Living as Men in Albania,"[7] we read about rural women who swear to remain virgins and thereby win the right to live as men in a deeply patriarchal culture plagued by wars and poverty. In families with no sons, daughters were a real liability, and so for centuries in Albania, some girls have grown up to be the "man of the house."

Other categories of gender variance, in central Asia, for example, distinguish carefully between the meaning of gender variance for a child, for teens, for marriageable males or females, and for individuals who have aged out of the marriage system. While global-gay discourses scoop up all signifiers of sex/gender difference into the net of "equal rights," presuming simple correspondence between legibility, identity, and recognition and rights and liberty, it becomes increasingly clear, in many places, that sexual tolerance is only used to free up new avenues for capital—and so, while gender-variant people in Thailand are tolerated only in certain circumstances, there has been a boom in surgical tourism in Bangkok, where transgender people can go to get their sex-reassignment surgeries for considerably less money than they would cost in the United States or Europe or Australia. Similarly, while there is mixed public support for gays and lesbians in Israel, tourist advertisements for Israel brand it as a vacation destination for gays and lesbians, a safe port in a stormy Middle Eastern landscape. And in the process of globalizing US-based models of sex and gender that are far from stable at "home," anthropologists, NGO workers, and grant agencies serve to prop up a system that is quietly and invisibly coming apart at the seams.

Some anthropologists who study sex/gender systems in other countries have been noticing and writing about the glaring differences between Euro-American ways of classifying sexual behaviors and classification systems that exist elsewhere. In a 2007 book, *Women's Sexualities and Masculinities in a Globalizing Asia*, editors Saskia Wieringa, Evelyn Blackwood, and Abha Bhaiya do propose to "decolonize global queer studies," by paying careful attention to the local forms of gender and sexuality regimes in Asia and by resisting the tendency to cast Asian sexualities as simple variations on the model of North American and European queer formulations. When we refuse to verify the seemingly inevitable *priorness* of US/European sexual economies, the volume promises to show, it becomes possible to recognize and learn from other modes of gender identification embedded in other kinds of sexual practice and productive of alternative forms of sociality and community and identity. The goal is commendable, to say the least, but the collection of essays itself has a hard time maintaining the localness of the US/European forms and an even harder time imagining the potential globality of Asian gender and sexual practices.

In her essay on women's same-sex practices in Japan, for example, Wieringa argues that "the Japanese language does not even have its own word for 'lesbian.'"[8] This idea that other languages should have a word that signifies female sexual variance in a way that corresponds to the English term "lesbian" repeats the very global hierarchy that the book says it wants to avoid by moving away from the term "queer." It also overlooks all the Japanese terms for sexual roles that we lack in English: *onabe*, for example. An onabe is a uniquely Japanese phenomenon. It is a word for biological women who pass as men (and in some cases who identify as male) and serve as "hosts" to mostly heterosexual women who come to visit the bars and nightclubs where they work. This is an almost unthinkable concept in English—straight women rarely visit with sex workers, and while we can perhaps accommodate images of heterosexual women being entertained by male erotic dancers at a hen party, the idea of straight women going out and paying for male companionship, whether from men or trans men, strikes most Americans as bizarre. But in Japan, where the influence of Christianity has been slight, we may find few women who call themselves "lesbian" but plenty of opportunities for women to hook up with trans men or with other women, and all of this may happen completely separate from any notion of a gay/lesbian/trans community.

When I visited Japan in 2004 and then again in 2010, I met lots of women who dated other women; some were gender variant, some were not. The bars were clustered in Shinjuku, and in one bar there were scores of "hostesses," cute feminine women dressed in chambermaid outfits and circulating in the club, selling cigarettes and . . . favors. Many of the queer people I met in Japan told me how frustrated they were when anthropologists would come and "study" them as if they were strange creatures in a zoo. They felt oppressed rather than liberated by the imposition of terms for gender and sexual variance that had been made popular in the United States and that were presumed to have universal applicability.

In Thailand, I had a similar kind of experience in the queer clubs. In fact, one night, after attending a queer-studies conference in Bangkok, some of us from the conference, including a female anthropologist who was working on lesbianism in Thailand, went to a bar. It was not easy to find, located on the very periphery of the city, down a small alleyway. Given the narrowness of the street, I presumed we would be walking into a very small club. Some of the clubs I had been to in Japan could accommodate no more than twenty-five people comfortably. Imagine my surprise, then, in Bangkok, when we walked into what felt like a massive town hall full of queer female types of people. The group with whom I arrived, mostly white, mostly androgynous academic lesbians, drifted to the margins of the hall and watched the action up on the stage, where a handsome "boy" or "tom," a masculine female-bodied person, was singing love songs while feminine women in the audience screamed. I was mesmerized by the scene and stood watching with my girlfriend of the time. Suddenly, a butch person approached me and said, "Come!" He gestured to me and my girlfriend to follow him, and we ended up standing around a small table with him and three cute feminine women. The butch slapped me heartily on the back and, pointing at me, said "Tom!" Basically, toms and dees were the names they used for the masculine and feminine partners in a "same sex" partnership. He pointed to my girlfriend and said, "Dee." Then he sent one of the young women at the table off to get me a drink and asked me what I wanted to sing up on the stage. Had I been a better singer, maybe I would have jumped and tried my best, just for the fun of it, but I declined and instead watched along with everyone else as one good-looking tom after another serenaded the crowd.

There must have been fifteen hundred to two thousand people in that club, despite the fact that Bangkok had felt singularly unqueer to me up until then. And while I was instantly readable to my table companions, my colleagues from the conference were not. Later, they asked me how I knew the people at the table—I explained that I didn't know them and that they didn't know me but that we all recognized each other. It does make a difference, in other words, when people are researching sex/gender systems,

whether they themselves are gender conforming or gender variant. The fact that the toms in the clubs in Bangkok recognized me
as a fellow tom made all the difference to our ability to feel comfortable together. Had I been conventionally gendered and gone
there looking for "lesbians," I would have been disappointed and
would have thought that the club was a throwback to the American '50s, a time when lesbians in the United States went secretly
to bars and dressed up as butches and femmes, sometimes because that was who they were, sometimes to pass. Seeing the club
in Bangkok as a version of something in the United States just
makes it seem "behind" and makes the US urban queer scenes,
with their "girl bars" and businesswomen gay clubs, seem modern by contrast.

While the tendency to read gender variance in non-Western
contexts as a sign of anachronism has not been particularly
productive, nor has the new tendency to read all gender variance as "transgenderism." This practice, fairly new given the
very recent rise in popularity of the term "transgender," has had
an immediate impact. When I was in Zagreb at a gender conference in October 2006, activists from Slovenia and Croatia
were complaining about having to use "transgender" in their
funding applications rather than any local terms for gender
variance. One presentation at the conference by activists from
Kyrgyzstan was about the different terms they use for gender-
variant people. The terms were determined by age as well as
by class status and degree of gender variance, and there were at
least four of them in use: the terms referenced the meaning of
gender variance at different ages, and so one word meant tom-
boy, another meant gender-variant adolescent, another meant
marriageable-age woman with signs of gender variance, and the
final term was used for women past the age of marriageability.
These terms were explained by the activists but then promptly

discarded in favor of the word "transgender." In making the switch to "transgender," the local terms and specific referencing of pre-marriage-age and post-marriage-age gender identities was lost. This is important, because the post-marriage-age categories implied a kind of free space for contrary gender and sexual identification. Once a female-bodied person is past her reproductive prime, these categories imply, the social scrutiny of her sexual activities and gender identification may lessen and s/he may experience a limited kind of freedom.

At any rate, the world is a big place; the systems we use in the United States and in Europe are neither natural nor inevitable, and around the world people have devised different systems to make gender and sexuality make sense. In the United States we have become far too sure about the stability and separation of various forms of gender and sexual identity. We are too confident about the operationality of the homo-hetero binary and the male/female divide, and because we are sure that these realms are separate, we do not think about how changes in one sphere create changes in other spheres: and so the momentous shifts in the meaning of gender and sex and sexuality that have allowed for the emergence of transgenders and transsexuals globally have also created massive, if unnoticed, shifts in the meaning of heterosexuality, male and female.

In fact, we need to think about sex and gender in a more ecological kind of framework, understanding that changes in one environment inevitably impact changes in other environments. Gender here might be thought of more as a climate or ecosystem and less as an identity or discrete bodily location. And so when we see sex/gender events like the pregnant man, like heteroflexibility, like metrosexuality, like gender fluidity, we are witnessing the aftershocks of the massive shifts that the emergence of transgenderism announced, presaged, and caused. Future shocks

are on the horizon, and instead of trying to prevent more damage, we should be hoping that one particularly powerful tremor
might bring the whole crumbling edifice of normative sex and
gender crumbling down.

HETEROFLEXIBILITY

One good place to look for signs of the end of normal is in those
locations where we presume that the normal is most stable. So
let's turn our attention to the heterosexual woman, who, after
all, so often has been forced to function as a model of conformity, a symbol of subjugation and the whipping girl for anything
that goes wrong with sexual morality. Gaga feminism is, above
all, concerned with reconfiguring the meaning of sex and gender
in ways that may favor heterosexual women in particular.

If we return to Daniel Bergner's article in the *New York
Times Magazine* on the flexibility of heterosexual female desires,
we will see that there and in his own book, Bergner seems to be
describing the wildness and unpredictability of sex, and so con-
tributing to the gaga project of scrambling completely the usual
coordinates for male/female, active/passive, masculine/feminine.
However, in his confidence in the solidity of the categories of
"male" and "female" and in his total belief in the stability of
heterosexuality, he undoes the premises of his own project—it is
as if he were smoothing with one hand the feathers he has just
ruffled with the other. Bergner encourages readers to wonder
about the "givens" in our sexual taxonomies while leading them
to other formulations altogether. At one point, however, he cites
queer psychologist Lisa M. Diamond, the author of a brave and
controversial book, *Sexual Fluidity*, which lays out a relatively
new theory of heteroflexibility. Diamond is more willing than
Bergner to build upon the premise of the instability of heterosexuality. She tries to prove that the classification systems that

we use for desire, love, and orientation do not work well for women, generally speaking, and so we need to grapple with the quite likely increasingly popular phenomenon of sexual fluidity over the course of a lifetime for increasing numbers of people.

Starting with quick examples from celebrity culture like Anne Heche, who dated men before and after her relationship with Ellen DeGeneres (no information about whether she also spoke "celestia" and came from another world before/after Ellen), or like Cynthia Nixon, the *Sex and the City* actress who left a fifteen-year relationship with a man for one with a woman in 2004, or other semicelebrities like Julie Cypher, who left a man for singer Melissa Etheridge and then went back to heterosexual dating afterward, Diamond shows that sexual orientation in some people ebbs and flows, moving between sexual objects and not necessarily settling on one kind of body or one set of sexual practices for ever and ever. Arguing that most models of sexual orientation are based on studies of men and male sexual preferences, Diamond proposes that we really don't know much about how female sexual response works over the course of a lifetime, and that the shuttling of desire between different orientations may be very common for women and may even define large swaths of what has been presumed to be female heterosexuality.

Generally speaking, when women do come out as gay later in life, there is a presumption that they were gay all along and just lacked the right environment to admit it. Or conversely, people might assume that, having failed with men, some women move on to try another group. When Meredith Baxter, the TV sitcom actress, came out in 2009, for example, the reasons that people ascribed to this later-life revelation, one that followed hard on the heels of three marriages, five children, accusations of domestic abuse against one husband, and a bout with breast cancer, were laden with assumptions about Baxter having been driven to lesbianism. But notice that when a woman stops dating other female-bodied people and takes up with a biological male, people then refer to her as "going back to heterosexuality," as if she had been on a short vacation, strayed away from her regular life but was now back on track. Women who are lesbians, then marry, then date women again, are rarely thought of as "going back to lesbianism," suggesting that lesbianism can never be either an origin or a destination—in other words, it can never be a primary mode of identification, nor can it be the goal a woman might shoot for.

These notions of orientation are saturated with assumptions about the normative, the right, the conventional. And if we go back to the late nineteenth century, the period when so many of these ideas about sexual conduct were first formed by doctors and lawyers and priests, we find that early ideas about lesbianism, circulated in the early twentieth century by Havelock Ellis and other sexologists, saw lesbianism as something that was congenital or inherent in some women (masculine women), but it was also generally understood that some women, feminine women, the partners of the masculine women, might choose lesbianism under certain dire circumstances. The only explanation that Ellis could produce for how and why this might happen was that these feminine lesbians were not very attractive and that they were women who had been rejected by men.

Nowadays, psychologists like Lisa Diamond are studying precisely this group of women, the feminine (and often very conventionally attractive) women who choose to be with other female-bodied people (who may in fact be masculine) rather than being with men (who sometimes may not be that masculine) and for whom this choice indicates a fluidity in their sexual wiring that flies in the face of most theories of sexual identity.

The idea that sexuality exists within the human body as a hard-wired system of settings—settings, moreover, that cannot be changed at will but that switch on and off in response to the subject's environment (cultural, social, and biological)—goes back to Freud, who believed that much of what we call human sexuality is established in an individual within the first few years of life. Because we receive all kinds of social and interpersonal imprinting at a very young age, often before we can even speak, by the time we reach puberty, our desires, our drives, our particular turn-ons and turn-offs have been established in our psyches in ways that are hard to change and may, in many cases, simply be permanent. This explains why, despite homophobic environments, gays and lesbians cannot, mostly, be converted "back" to heterosexuality. It explains why there is no such thing as an original heterosexuality from which the person deviates ("perversion" means the swerving away from one path and onto another). But, by Freud's own admission, he modeled his understanding of human sexuality on male embodiment, and felt that the application of his theories of desire, stages of development, taboos, and repression must work differently for women. Freud famously asked "What do women want?" probably more out of exasperation than curiosity.

Diamond begins with this premise and goes on to propose that male and female orientation in terms of desire is very different, and that "one of the fundamental, defining features of female sexual orientation is its *fluidity*."[9] I think this is a valid and important claim, but I would want to supplement it by recognizing that for other people, some of whom are female, sexual fluidity will *not* characterize the ebbs and flows of their desires and sexual practices. Some women may be completely committed, psychically speaking, to desiring male bodies and only male bodies. Some may be clitorally focused, others may be vaginally focused, some may change focus after experiencing childbirth, finding that their desires and their genitalia work differently after pushing out a seven-pound baby.

In fact, it may well be that certain forms of femininity (in men and women) are defined by flexibility and fluidity while certain forms of masculinity (in men and women) are defined as fixed and rigid. And so, for example, in relation to lesbian sexualities, the category we call "butch" is quite identified with sexual fixity in many cases, and the appellation of the category "stone butch" actually names that fixity: stone butch generally means a totally masculine woman, or a very masculine lesbian, and it also indicates a disinclination for penetration. Of course, many men are also "stone"—they have orifices (the anus, for example) that could be penetrated, but they define their sexuality in opposition to penetrability and understand themselves as penetrating instead.

On this front (or back, as the case may be), all these new youth vampire films like the Twilight series capitalize on the versatility of vampire desires across different bodies—male and female vampires both penetrate and are penetrated. Meanwhile, back in the mundane real world, men tend to think of themselves as those sexual agents who penetrate others, and women tend to think of themselves, or at least they get characterized, as bodies to be penetrated. If some masculine women think of themselves as penetrators rather than penetratees, then we speak in terms of pathology and we name that category in terms of its resistance to norms. We do not speak of stone men, but we do think in terms of "stone butches": this allows for butches to be caricatured as rigid or immobile or frozen. The popular lesbian expression "melting the stone" actually implies that stoneness, an immobile set of relations between desire, embodiment, femaleness, and masculinity, needs to be and can be thawed through the right combination of intimacy, love, and connection. Some bodies don't want to thaw, however; some do not want to be fluid or transitional; some will always occupy a place of resistance to notions of flexibility and pliability, especially as they become dominant.

Male desire, gay and straight, despite its often phobic insistence on fixity, is almost never characterized as pathological. For example, in the research reported in the aforementioned *New York Times Magazine* article, male desire conformed to expectations—heterosexual men were turned on only by women, and homosexual men only by men. The fact that male desire cannot be switched on and off by multiple narratives or contexts but functions in very literal ways as a primal response to gendered bodies is hardly ever cast as a problem—when butches incorporate similar versions of masculinity to the heterosexual male, we speak in terms of inflexibility and inability to perform receptiveness. In some gay men, the absolute erotic rejection of femininity, whether it is found in other men or in women, in drag queens or in fag hags, is again never cast as a mode of sexual dysfunction.

In other words, people are not asking why it is that gay men do not, generally speaking, produce any fantasies around femininity, while lesbians produce lots of fantasy environments that include men or masculinity. When, in *The Kids Are All Right*, the lesbian couple watches gay male pornography to spice up their sex life, the scene was met with incredulity, especially from gay men. Indeed, a gay magazine journalist called me and asked me to comment on this bizarre (to him) scene. I responded that lots of lesbians watch and like gay male porn, straight male porn, and everything in between, and I asked him whether he thought gay men also watched a wide range of pornographic material. He responded in the negative and turned hostile when I suggested that this was what he should write about: why can gay men, generally speaking, *only* activate desire in relation to the representation of gay male scenarios and never through fantasies involving women or femininity?

So, to recap, while men, gay and straight, tend to respond in inflexible ways to erotic images of men and women (straight men want to see female bodies, gay men want to see male bodies), women, gay and straight, tend to respond in flexible ways to images of men, women, and animals. When inflexibility does occur in female desire (a disinclination for penetration, say), we speak of pathological fixity. When inflexibility appears in male desire (a disinclination for penetration, say), we speak of a normal range of erotic interest. While the heterosexual male's disinterest in seeing any male bodies in his erotic landscapes could be attributed to homophobia, and while the homosexual male's disinterest in seeing any female bodies in his erotic landscapes could be attributed to misogyny, we still code both sets of disinclinations as rational, normal, obvious. When flexibility seems to characterize female desires, we confess to being baffled.

As we ponder the potentially misogynist exclusivity of gay male desire and the potentially homophobic exclusivity of straight male desire, let's now also ask what happens when heterosexual men express or try to express flexibility. Let me start with an anecdote (real story): A guy calls me from *New York Magazine:* "I want to talk to you about men's underwear," he says. OK, this is pretty standard fare for a gender studies professor, one has to go with the flow, answer questions on everything from pregnant men to pink Power Rangers. I can think about men's underwear. What's up? Well, says my reporter guy, I go in the bathroom the other day in my new briefs that my girlfriend has bought me and I realize . . . is this OK? he asks hesitantly . . . Yeah, sure, I respond. Your new briefs, you are in the bathroom . . . go on. Well, he says, I get up to the urinal and I realize the briefs have no opening and so I cannot really get myself in position to pee without pulling everything down, so I have to use the stall, which is, you know, embarrassing . . . Yes, I see, I say. So, what's up with that? We go on to have a great discussion about designer briefs, changing notions of masculinity, the packaging of the male body in such a way that studliness is, well, "enhanced" while usefulness is eradicated. I ask him if he has heard of the performance artist Peggy Shaw, who, in a great piece about her own masculinity titled *Just Like My Father*, says she prefers men's underwear to women's because "they have a logic." Exactly, says my reporter friend, men's briefs do have a logic, but now the logic of use has been replaced with the logic of size.

Indeed, the horrible slogan "Size Does Matter" and the appearance on coffee tables of tomes like *The Big Penis Book*[10] really do require some kind of explanation. At first glance, the size-does-matter argument seems to be a bodily metaphor for the kinds of military operations that the United States invested in during the same period that men's briefs switched from tighty-whities to package enhancers. But this seems too easy. Could it be that a new age of informality about sexuality allowed for men and women to discuss what has been a whispered conversation all along? Is it the case that for most women who are really into undetachable penises, bigger is sexier? Aren't there surely some women for whom large penises are unwieldy or painful to . . . um . . . accommodate? Is this a slippage between gay male cultures and straight cultures, a consequence of the gay man–fag hag bond within which the gay male focus on dick size trickles down to women who may or may not desire very large penises? Finally, in an age of breast enhancement, are penises and breasts coming in ungainly and unnaturally large sizes and then creating a demand for size, or does the supersizing follow some other logic, a marketplace logic of bigger is better? Well, until women who like smaller penises and men who have smaller penises begin talking about it, we may never know. I know a pushy feminine woman who likes to say, very loudly in public, and usually when her husband is present: "What's the big deal? The difference between men and women comes down to a lousy four-inch appendage!" As everyone laughs uproariously, her husband always waits for a minute and then says, quietly, "Six inches, six!" Size does matter, but should it always matter in a way that favors girth? A femme friend who dates short butch women had a T-shirt made recently: "I heart pocket butches." Some people like it small.

Mr. Journalism and I actually had a very easy rapport when talking together about things that usually only guys talk about. I told him that I preferred men's underwear and why; I asked him about his dating practices; and he accepted the idea of talking to a butch as reasonable and perhaps even preferable to talking to a bio guy. In fact, he recognized, perhaps in ways that many straight women are less apt to, that a lot has changed in the world of gender and sexuality in the last few decades and that his underwear was trying to tell him something. He was, in a sense, the guy described in Susan Faludi's great book, *Stiffed: The Betrayal of the Modern Man*,[11] the potentially feminist male who realizes that if heterosexual women needed feminism in order to navigate a toxic terrain of male privilege, heterosexual men need their own gender politics to understand the shifty landscapes of manhood and masculinity.

When they are not trying to figure out how to pee standing up while looking studly in package-enhancing briefs, bio men have other problems to sort out. Being a man in the age of sexual fluidity is no mean feat, and while the straight ladies are buzzing off together, the lonely dudes are dodging their whiny would-be wives and wondering whether there is a pill for going gay. Not really, but the old "just guys" thing doesn't really work anymore, and yet no one likes a sensitive man, mouthing some truism he overheard his wife say while sneaking off to watch Internet porn.

Men, in general, would do well to learn from butches how to see their masculinity as culturally constructed, contingent, and hard-won. I hoped that this was what was happening in a recent art show that came to my attention, called *Butch Craft*. This show, curated by Murray Moss in New York City and written up by Penelope Green in the *New York Times*,[12] attempts to return masculinity to aesthetics and the act of making to an increasingly abstracted art world. Green, to her great credit, tried to excavate the relations between "butch" as a term coined for masculine lesbians and "butch" as a catchall marker for everything masculine. But the boys do not want to consent to the idea that their masculinity might derive from, collaborate with, or be influenced by any kind of queer subculture, and so Moss bats away all suggestions of derivation and says simply: "I used the term 'butch,' versus 'masculine' or 'tough' or 'manly,' because what I mean by this is work that is stereotypically considered manly, but expressed by a personality that is stereotypically considered sensitive or feminine."[13] And so, men get to have their cake and eat it too—play the artist while holding onto their virility; mark their masculinity as different without ever putting themselves in a dangerous proximity to the queer. But more and more, in an increasingly confusing and confused world of gender and sexual upheavals, cultural narratives of masculinity do not depend upon such repudiations. Let's look at a charming example of one narrative about masculinity that recognizes the butch in the man, the man in the butch, and the fox in us all.

FANTASTIC MR. FOX LOSES HIS TAIL

The 2009 animated film *Fantastic Mr. Fox* tells the story of a fox family, Mr. Fox (voiced by George Clooney) and his wife, Mrs. Fox (Meryl Streep), their son Ash (Jason Schwartzman) and his cousin Kristofferson (Eric Anderson). Each member of the family is striving for something more, some alternative way of being in a world that is overly preoccupied with the straight and narrow. Like much of director Wes Anderson's work, this film makes eccentricity into a way of life, exploring alternatives that pop up in the everyday, and it does so by using the slightly sinister barebones of a Roald Dahl story about three mean farmers and the fox that tries to outwit them. In the story, a children's song provides the mise-en-scène:

> Boggis and Bunce and Bean
> One fat, one short, one lean
> These horrible crooks
> So different in looks
> Were nonetheless equally mean.

The mean farmers provide a scary backdrop to the narrative about Mr. Fox's struggle with his masculinity. Finding domesticity in the fox burrow to be a tad too, well, tame, Mr. Fox goes back to stealing chickens from the farmers. He also engages in some Oedipal rivalry with his son, who is locked in a mortal battle of sibling rivalry with his immaculate and talented cousin Kristofferson. Just as the film seems like it is going to be an all-male testosterone fest of competition, one-upmanship, and violence, it tips into something else altogether. Aided by the wonder of stop-motion animation, a form that never lets the viewer forget that they are watching a magical construction of movement and color, *Fantastic Mr. Fox* turns into an allegory of modern masculinity, its trials and tribulations.

In one violent and traumatic encounter with the farmers, Mr. Fox loses his tail. Literally. He loses his bushy symbol of manhood and returns to the burrow with chickens but without one of the markers of his unique masculinity. Rather than becoming impotent, anxious, downhearted or defeated, however, Mr. Fox makes do. He improvises, learns to live without the appendage, and waits patiently until, in the film's denouement, his son, Ash, a sissy boy who wears lipstick and shies away from masculine pursuits, recaptures the tail (which one of the farmers was wearing as a tie!) and returns it triumphantly to his father. This seals the relation between the father and the son without excluding or demeaning Kristofferson, and Mr. Fox tells his family that he is happy to have a detachable tail—it is now pinned to his derriere and can be taken off or put on at will. Getting his tail back but in a new form releases Mr. Fox from his phallic burden to, as he archly puts it, "always be the quote unquote 'fantastic Mr. Fox'"—now he can just alternate as he likes between fantastic and wild, wild and reliable, wise and reckless. The shift away from phallic power also allows him to embrace his sissy son Ash, who wears dresses and feels he can never earn his father's respect for his own masculinity. Ash in a dress may be better off than his father in the brave new world of gender fluidity that seems to wipe the ground with these neuroses about marriage, underwear, and who wears the tail.

Fantastic Mr. Fox is a queerly animated classic about a tailless male in a world of phallic power. And it confirms for us all—butches, femmes, trans men, wild animals, foxes alike—that detachable tails may be in fashion, gender categories always threaten to run wild, and with every shift and change in cultural meanings and mores, endless new possibilities emerge for love, life, and liberation.

FOUR

Gaga Relations:
The End of Marriage

*It destroys one's nerves to be amiable everyday to the
same human being.*

—Benjamin Disraeli

*Love, the strongest and deepest element in all life, the
harbinger of hope, of joy, of ecstasy; love, the defier
of laws, of all conventions; love, the freest, the most
powerful molder of human destiny; how can such an
all-compelling force be synonymous with that poor
little State- and Church-begotten weed, marriage?*

—Emma Goldman

Remember, licking doorknobs is illegal on other planets!

—SpongeBob SquarePants

RSVP

Why is it that whenever you have a big, heated argument with
someone who wants you to relent on your critique of gay marriage, they turn around and invite you to their big fat gay wedding? Just recently this happened to me . . . again. The first
time was during one of those brief periods when it was, by fiat
of the mayor, legal for a minute for gay people to get married
in San Francisco. A longtime former friend, actually the same
friend who moved out of the Castro once she and her girlfriend

had kids because they were worried about the potential harm to their children of sexual imagery in the store windows there, sent around a wedding notice listing all the reasons that she and her fabulously wealthy girlfriend were getting married and then inviting everyone to a wedding and directing them to a gift registry. Number one on this list of reasons to get married, it turned out, was the super-romantic rationale of the hallowed tax benefit. Despite the fact that some financial advisers now say that marriage does not necessarily lead to a more robust household economy, this argument—that gays and lesbians should be allowed to get married so that they can access tax benefits like heterosexual couples—has remarkable power and endurance. Perhaps only in the United States, where taxes are treated like theft rather than seen as part of a social project designed to keep money flowing through the system, and where many large corporations manage to pay very little in taxes because they hire lawyers to spring them from such tiresome obligations, can the phrase "tax benefits" ring forth like a liberation anthem.

Another friend also engaged me in some light banter about marriage and love and then, after a provocative response from me, turned around and invited me to his very expensive wedding. This friend was a longtime marriage opponent who, sometime in the last five years, transitioned from female to male, began living as a man, and hooked up with a woman with two kids. Newly minted as a family man, this friend immediately wanted to get married. Shocked by this turnaround, I questioned my friend and his new fiancée about their need to marry when he had just transitioned into manhood and she had, after all, just transitioned out of heterosexuality.

When we met for dinner to discuss their upcoming nuptials, the conversation quickly became awkward. Sporting freshly inked tattoos with the dates of their engagement inscribed on their arms, the couple positively glowed. While they displayed their tattoos, I recalled the last time my friend had tattooed a lady's name on his arm before dumping her unceremoniously a year or two later and wondered what would be so different this time. Let me be clear: I don't require proof that people are going to stay together forever in order to coo over their love tattoos. But I also don't expect to be called up to witness their promise to stay together forever and ever in a rather pricey and pretentious wedding ceremony. I especially don't expect to be invited to sign up for a registry where they have posted lists of startlingly expensive gifts. While gay, lesbian, and trans people may think that, by tying the knot and going legal, they are changing a very old and conventional institution, be warned: *before you change it, it changes you.*

OK, so I am grumpy about gay marriage. Ask the poor guy who stopped me in the street the other day, trying to get me to sign his petition for legalizing gay marriage in the state of California. "Don't you have anything better to do with your political energies?" I snapped. He looked startled, having pegged me for sure as queer in some way and therefore bound to support his cause. The street activist's absolute confidence that I would be a supporter of gay marriage, just like the certainty with which all my former friends invite me to their weddings assuming that I will finally see the light, implies that, generally speaking, the critique of gay marriage has not been well articulated in the public sphere. Instead, think tanks like the Williams Institute have dominated the airwaves with their rights-advocacy arguments, and all the opposition to gay marriage has been depicted as external to queer communities and as coming from Christian fundamentalist groups. However, there is a fierce and powerful argument against gay marriage from *within* queer activist groups, and it is time for it to be heard within a larger, left-leaning conversation among queers about social responsibility, social justice, and the potential connections between radical queers and other radical groups in the culture at large.

FROM HOMO TO GAY AND BACK AGAIN

Without getting too academic about this, it's important to understand the activist emphasis on marriage within a much longer history of homo/sexuality. Gay marriage as an activist target seems to complete a long process of human classification that began in the late nineteenth century and is ongoing today. This process that began by making fundamental assumptions about human difference by distinguishing between people with homo and people with hetero desires comes full circle when homo people ask to be recognized just like hetero people.

One theorist, Michel Foucault, someone who has greatly influenced the ways that academics write and think about sex, linked the emergence of the category of "homosexual" (1869) to the onset of industrialization, the rise of a culture of expertise (a medical culture then but nowadays more of a talk show culture—think Dr. Phil and self-help literature), the increasing intrusion of medical terms into everyday modes of identifying oneself, and the fragmentation of society/groups/families into people/individuals/subjects: these developments, many people agree, are the hallmarks of the modern world.

Foucault did not stop there, however; he also proposed that a transition occurs between seeing people as part of a group or class and as engaged in actions or practices to seeing folks as defined by hardwired identities and as separate selves. This process begins in the medical lab or the therapist's office but it is only confirmed when the very people whom the doctors are busily classifying actually begin to think of themselves in those terms: while doctors and psychologists might have agreed upon definitions of "normal" and "perverse," those definitions do not take on a sense of permanence and inevitability until someone actually identifies with the terms.

So, while in the 1910s an effeminate man in New York City who has sex with other men may think of himself as a "fairy" may not have ruled out the possibility of marrying a woman, and may consider himself as harboring a vice or as sinning against God, some twenty or thirty years later, a similar kind of man may think of himself as incurably homosexual, as doomed to a life of loneliness and stigma and as someone whom society has marginalized and cast as a pedophile. He will certainly think of himself as having a homosexual identity and may be seeking psychiatric help. Evidence for this framework can be found in the many films of the 1930s to 1960s that depict male homosexuality in precisely these terms—as sad, compulsive, pathological, and antisocial. Such films—like Alfred Hitchcock's *Rope* (1948), Richard Brooks's *Cat on a Hot Tin Roof* (1958), Basil Dearden's *Victim* (1961), and John Huston's *Reflections in a Golden Eye* (1967)—never had to name the sin they depicted (they literally could not name it, because the Hays Code, enforced to control media influence, forbade the depiction of homosexuality); they merely had to indicate that there was something "unmentionable" about the pathology from which the main character suffers.

And by the 1970s, a similar man will think of himself as gay, out, proud; he may be super invested in his masculinity and may resist the categories of "fairy" or "homosexual" altogether and think of his identification with the term "gay" as liberatory! So how, you might ask, did we begin with a diagnosis, move through social marginalization, and arrive at gay pride and gay marriage? But even if you don't ask, you might want to ask, because the struggles that people endured before us have often afforded us our sense of "liberation." And what is more, other political trajectories would have led to other kinds of goals for liberation.

Indeed, the desire for marriage completes a long process by which LGBT people, having been separated out from normative society and called pathological, now are embraced and in turn embrace the very cultures that previously rejected them. In fact, I would take this point further: the participation of LGBT couples in state-sanctioned marriages lends credibility to the very institution that has acquired meaning precisely through excluding gays and lesbians, among others, from marriage in the first place. In other words, marriage has been an exclusionary system rather than an inclusionary one; it has functioned precisely by drawing lines between those who can and those who cannot legally marry. In the twentieth century, people who have been prohibited from marrying include gays, lesbians, trans people, and mixed-race couples. An institution that has been defined through such exclusions and that has been enforced as a system of class alliance, of racial purity, of religious sanction, should surely be dismantled rather than expanded!

Just as new classifications (medical and psychological) of personhood at the end of the nineteenth century created "homosexual" people and "heterosexual" people, they also, through a kind of conceptual sleight of hand, forced people to speak about homo- and heterosexuals, men and women, as if they belonged to different species and as if the differences between each group was distinct, clear, and, above all, natural. One legacy of this division of sexualities and genders into "separate species," has been a lasting inability to see connections when we might want to make more general statements about shifts and changes in gender and sexuality across the culture. And so we speak of gay and lesbian history as if there is one single narrative for all lesbians and all gay men and as if that narrative has coherence and unfolds in terms of exclusion and marginalization followed by protests and revolts and then resolves in terms of accommodation and assimilation. But of course, history unfolds along very different lines for people in different classes, people in different racial groups, and people of different genders. Gay male history does not line up nicely with lesbian history; black histories of sexuality look very different from white ones; histories involving queer people who emigrate from one region to another look massively different from histories of people who spend their whole lives in one area, one city, one neighborhood, even.

Scholars have grappled for years with the challenge of mapping these very disparate differences, and so, too often, one history, a history of white gay men, has come to represent all of gay, lesbian, and transgender history. Why? Because there are paper trails for gay male history that are missing for other histories—gay men have been legally prosecuted, tried, convicted, and sentenced to prison (Oscar Wilde's famous trial, for example, in the late nineteenth century); gay male history has intersected with the histories of dominant culture, but lesbian and trans histories tend to leave less archival material and less traces. For this reason, conventional histories of sexual minorities often take the form of focusing on one event (Stonewall) and then turning it into a representative moment. And so while the history of early twenty-first century LGBT politics will inevitably get told later as a story of the struggle for gay marriage, gay marriage is merely a part of the much more diverse and radical fabric of queer activism, and it may not even be the most popular cause for gays and lesbians and trans people. It has become the most visible, however, because its goals mesh well with the status quo and they seem to confirm the rightness of the social values in which heterosexuals have chosen to invest.

And gay marriage may have very different meaning for different queer communities: as even the Williams Institute studies make clear, gay marriage will do little for queer people currently living in poverty, while it has definite tax benefits for the middle class and the very rich. The hallmark of post–World War II LGBT social movements has tended to be the attempt to change society, to model a different way of relating, of cohabiting, of desiring. So how did we arrive at this historical juncture where an assimilationist politics of marriage now stands in for all queer political aspiration? Many queers today still believe in social movements far less focused on marriage equality and far more interested in changing the structures of intimate modes of relating, belonging, and cohabiting altogether. Many activists outside of the mainstream LGBT marriage-equality movement try to make connections between homophobia and other forms of social and political exclusion. Not content to slip smoothly into already existing corrupt and bankrupt institutions, radical queers still hold on to the idea that something lies "beyond marriage" (as one group calls itself), and, moreover, that human difference should flourish not in the rounding out of existing structures but in the creative invention of new ones.

THE CASE AGAINST GAY MARRIAGE

Let's discuss a more imaginative kind of activism, one that is less tied to a politics of respectability, one that is more committed to change and transformation, and one that is less invested in maintaining US social institutions as they have been formulated in relation to racist and homophobic commitments. I want to summarize quickly the opposition to gay marriage as formulated by progressive or left-leaning groups such as Beyond Gay Marriage, think about the question posed in a number of conversations as to whether "gay marriage is racist" or even specifically "anti-black," and then end with some speculations on activism less focused on changing laws and more intent upon the transformation of social, psychic, and political worlds. At stake here are questions about what counts as political in any given context, oppositions between pragmatism and utopianism, and more questions about how to argue for change, how to recognize change when it actually occurs, and how to think about political pasts, presents, and futures in ways that do not simply produce a sense of political inevitability.

As I have said, not all queer people are advocates of gay marriage; indeed, according to some activist groups, for most queer people this is not their main political priority. In mainstream political circles, however, gay marriage has become the cause célèbre and has come to stand in for gay and lesbian politics as a whole. Any heterosexual celebrity who wants to be seen as an ally to LGBT communities will stick the gay-marriage feather in his or her cap as a sign of solidarity. Indeed, Lady Gaga has dedicated public appearances to giving speeches calling for marriage equality, as she did for the repeal of Don't Ask, Don't Tell. While this only adds to her appeal to white gay men in particular, it reminds us that we should not confuse the representational mayhem that Lady Gaga has been able to wreak in her videos with her actual politics. I am not saying that Lady Gaga should stop talking about gay causes, but I am saying that what makes her interesting, what makes her gaga, has very little to do with the clichéd political positions she takes. In other words, while it is brave to stand up and speak on behalf of sexual minorities, and while it is important, especially to young people, for fans to see their idols support meaningful causes, it is still the case that actions and words are two very different things. And while Lady Gaga's words in political speeches are ordinary, her performances, her costumes, her gestures, the worlds she creates and peoples are extraordinary. For this reason, I build gaga feminism on the bedrock of the outrageous performance archive that Lady Gaga has created and not in relation to her speeches on behalf of marriage equality or gays in the military, positions that offer no critique of marriage on the one hand or the military on the other.

So, for Lady Gaga and others who wonder why some queer people actually oppose gay marriage, consider the following points.

Reactive Politics Are Weak Politics

Gay marriage has become a central issue partly because right-wing Christian groups mount such a furious opposition to it. In other words, "we" have made it into a big issue because "they" have made it into a big issue—the politics around gay marriage, then, in part is reactive rather than proactive. Reactive politics are weak and defensive, are defined by the opposition, and tend to retreat into justifications instead of moving forward through provocations. Furthermore, marriage-equality movements have the unfortunate tendency to bolster other conservative marriage movements, often Christian, by lending credibility to a failing arrangement in its hour of need.

Inclusion Maintains the Status Quo

Gay marriage is being formulated by legal-reform groups as a "stand-alone" issue, it tends not to be linked to other social justice projects, and it borrows heavily from a civil rights–era "rights" discourse around inclusion and extension of the status quo. Making marriage into a stand-alone issue actually makes nonsense of the comparison to civil rights struggles. While the civil rights struggles against institutionalized racism sought to transform the whole society, the marriage-equality activists seek to maintain the status quo while demanding a bigger slice of the pie. When gay people get married, keep in mind, they may well extend the institution of marriage, but they do not change it. What is more, while many marriage activists make the analogy to civil rights struggles, much of the white gay-marriage leadership make no connections between race and sexuality and few overtures to communities of color harboring misgivings about gay marriage. Indeed, the "white" agenda of gay-marriage advocates may have contributed to large numbers of African American and Latino/a voters casting their votes against the repeal of Prop. 8 in the 2008 elections.

In some popular media, gay marriage is depicted as a black-and-white issue, with white gays wanting to get married and black Christians opposing them. The opposition to gay marriage is all too often read monolithically as part and parcel of right-wing moral outrage and a "values" agenda when in fact people from different backgrounds may have different reasons for opposing not simply gay marriage but what it represents in terms of the landscape of political action in the United States. For black families that have long been represented as dysfunctional, and that have been destabilized by prison expansion and welfare reform, many of the so-called rights attached to marriage have not necessarily benefited them. As feminist and queer scholar Priya Kandaswamy put it in an interview published in 2004: "While many of its advocates argue that gay marriage would secure parental rights for gay and lesbian couples, I think this actually depends on a lot more than marital status. In the US, race is the strongest determinant of whether or not the state chooses to recognize your parental ties. Black families are the most likely of any racial group to be disrupted by Child Protection authorities and 42% of all children in foster care in the US are black. If being married does not protect straight black families from having their children taken away, it's unlikely it will protect queer black families."[1]

Black communities are also sometimes angered by simple comparisons between gay-marital-equality struggles and black civil rights battles—gay mainstream groups catering to white people have used this language of comparison without any accompanying attention to racism within white gay and lesbian communities or to poverty issues or health care issues for people of color, and the mainstream groups pushing for marriage almost never link their struggle to other social justice issues like prison reform. And marriage is not the only arena where white gays and lesbians seem to be locked in a struggle for political credibility with communities of color.

For example, one film, *Flag Wars*, a documentary from 2003 by Linda Goode Bryant and Laura Poitras, has documented the ways in which black communities get pitted against gay and lesbian white home-owners, with the gay and lesbian realtors and buyers trying to access property and gentrify, while the local black communities face housing discrimination and redlining. The film tells a rather unwelcome story about the impact of gentrification, portraying white gays and lesbians as part of the system that economically oppresses people of color rather than as people who share in the experience of marginalization. The film depicts a warts-and-all confrontation between house-proud gentrifiers and long-term residents, renters, in the neighborhood. The white home-buyers, though never overtly racist, fail to appreciate, whether deliberately or not, the impact that they are having on a historically black neighborhood. And they never link their own experience with oppression to the economic disenfranchisement that they see all around them.

Queer historian Christina Hanhardt writes about these clashes between white gay and lesbian liberation struggles and the political and economic struggles of communities of color in a forthcoming book. Showing that early gay-liberation movements in New York, San Francisco, and Los Angeles, in the 1960s and 1970s, all began with big, broad, lofty goals for social justice that linked them to communities of color and made little separation between antipoverty struggles, antiracist agendas, and gay-rights projects, Hanhardt charts the ways in which white gay and lesbian groups quickly switched tacks and began to name their politics in terms of "antiviolence." Where once these groups made strong alliances with impoverished communities of color, later they focused in on homophobia, and, fearing homophobic violence, they called for more police presence and more protection on the street, and many of them set about gentrifying some of the poorer neighborhoods (in San Francisco this happened in the Western Addition, for example). This drive to make the streets safe for white queer people resulted all too often in increased policing for people of color.

So, as even these brief examples show, there are good reasons for communities of color to mistrust affluent white gays, and there are also at the same time many communities of color who support queer politics but oppose gay marriage for the same reasons that many black queer activists oppose it. And of course, I am not at all suggesting here that gays and lesbians are white and communities of color are straight, I am rather trying to unpack the complex racial politics at work in these struggles that get represented as streamlined and simple. The main problem with a politics of inclusion, where a group of people seek to be folded into existing institutions like marriage, ultimately lies with the economic divisions that marriage politics ignore. Marriage remains an issue that appeals to affluent white gays and lesbians who will benefit from it. It has far less appeal to queers living in poverty or queers actively working on social justice issues that stretch beyond securing individual benefits or tax breaks.

Rights Should Not Be Marriage-Dependent

The push to extend some of the partnership rights covered by marriage to those couples who could not or chose not to marry began in the 1980s and resulted in domestic-partnership ordinances in many cities. These measures did not allow unmarried couples to access all of the benefits that they might have secured through marriage, but domestic partnership did serve as a useful alternative to marriage, and it also gave traditional-marriage resisters a way to register their relationships with the state. As Nancy D. Polikoff comments in her astute book *Beyond (Straight and Gay) Marriage,* the problem for many couples seeking to secure health benefits, however, cannot be resolved through either marriage or domestic partnership. Only universal health coverage would really allow everyone access to the benefits that some people seek through marriage and civil unions. Polikoff provides a quick historical sketch of how the United States came to bundle health insurance into employment pay packages rather than structuring it as a universally accessible system. She reminds us that concepts like the "family wage," which emerged in the nineteenth century, assumed that men earned the money and then shared their resources with their wives and children in ways that made women and children structurally dependent upon men. Polikoff writes: "Consistent with the concept of the family wage, when benefits became a part of employee compensation, employers took into account a worker's responsibility to support his wife and children. Women presumed not to have such needs, did not receive equal benefits."[2]

Arguing that as family forms have changed—more women have entered the workplace, more marriages have ended in divorce, more elderly people have moved in with their middle-aged children, and so on—so too should the system that assigns benefits and access to health care. Polikoff is succinct in her evaluation of the present state of health benefits, and she proposes adjusting "eligibility to reflect today's families," adding, as she explains why employers should cover all the diverse forms that families take now, that "marriage should not be required." There is no better way to say it—marriage and domestic partnerships should not be required in the first place in order for partners and children and dependents to access adequate health care.

Alternative Intimacies Are Not Served by the Marriage Model

There are many ways of creating family, kinship, intimacy, and community that exceed the marriage model. Some of these may include: shared parenting arrangements, split families, communities living together without children, and, last but certainly not least, threesomes. (A Los Angeles group called the Toxic Titties developed a fabulous performance piece where they sought to be married as three people.) The privileging of long-term, permanent arrangements between couples, especially those that include childrearing, grants priority to forms of relation that can be tracked and documented over forms of relation that are ephemeral and temporary. Given that there can easily be more intimacy in an occasional relationship with spark and passion than in an inert domestic partnership that has long outlived its original intensity, why value one over the other when it comes to social stability, or happiness, or the benefit of children?

One of the most compelling reasons given to push for gay marriage, as mentioned above, has been the access to health and other benefits that marriage would confer upon gay as well as straight couples. But again, as I note above, this issue can be approached and resolved in other ways, and in its privileging of marriage, it calls attention to the way we value some forms of social connection over other equally valid ones. Polikoff's work, again, is very useful here, as she gives the legal perspective on why marriage equality is not the solution for working toward the recognition of diverse households. Polikoff comments:

> An employer should not protect only partners of employ-ees whose relationships have been granted formal status by the state. The principles behind making marriage mat-ter less that animated early domestic partnership policies still apply. Given the vast increase in couples living together without marrying, in the context of a legal system that has made getting married and staying married more optional, there is no basis for requiring marriage or its same-sex ana-logue for someone to count as a family member.[3]

For example, one could argue that everyone should have the option to extend their benefits packages to others, to a "plus one" instead of verifiable relatives. If the guy in the office next to me has five kids with three different women and can add any of these kids to his medical insurance, why can't I sign up the old lady who lives next door and who watches my apartment for me when I am gone? Or the man down the street who is between jobs but does odd jobs around the neighborhood? Why not have a system where anyone can pay for up to six others as a "family"? Why not value forged connection as much as blood in terms of ways we think about belonging? We could argue that these "alternative intimacies" would make society much stronger and in much more elaborate ways than marriage does. Marriage pits the family and the couple against everyone else; alternative intimacies stretch connections between people and across neighborhoods like invisible webs, and they bind us to one another in ways that foster communication, responsibility, and generosity. If we are really committed to making life better for as many people as possible, then we should consider replacing marriage with wider units of connection and relation.

And in fact, new family arrangements involving gender-variant partners in queer relationships are changing the sex/gender styles and beliefs of a whole new generation, and it is quite possible that within our lifetimes, gays and lesbians and LGBT families will become as ubiquitous and as accepted as divorced households and that divorced households will lose their stigma and simply be seen as a practical way of raising children outside of nuclearity. The goal here, then, should be to recognize the variety within which households can come—the diversity of domestic relations, the inventiveness of human connection, and not the singling out of one form of relation (coupledom, marriage) over all others.

Marriage Is an Oppressive Ideology

In terms of principled opposition to gay marriage, some queer scholars have tried to expose the ways in which young people are led to believe that marriage and babies represent the only possible future within which they can live out their adult desires. And so, we lead young girls in particular to believe that they will be swept naturally along from one life-defining event to another—that love leads to marriage, marriage to babies, babies to family contentment, and that once in the shelter of the family, life will be sweet, simple, and fulfilling. And for some people, fairy tales really do come true. But for most of us, the arc along which our lives will play out will be considerably more complicated than this normal timeline implies. There will be stops and starts, ups and downs, and the family, rather than a sanctuary, may for many be a kind of prison that we assiduously avoid.

I read a story in a magazine a few years ago about a guy, a young man, handsome and on his way to a successful career, who was missing one thing in his life: a wife. His parents were deeply disappointed in him, dismayed that he could go forward in life without a (female) partner. The young man started dating; became serious about a young woman; proposed to her; and walked out on her the day before their wedding. His therapist diagnosed him as suffering from a fear of intimacy, and his parents were hurt and bewildered. The guy eventually left the United States altogether and went to live in Germany, alone; he never married and was totally happy without a partner. While the magazine story used this man to think through intimacy disorders, it is quite possible that there is no disorder here at all—only a perfectly reasonable desire to be alone, to live alone, to avoid intimacy where intimacy is so tethered to a one-size-fits-all format of cohabitation and marriage.

Marriage, the supposedly "big" event in the life of a young person, is, as so many feminists have pointed out, as much of an ending as a beginning (as Jane Eyre states quietly at the end of the famed eponymous novel about looking for love in all the wrong places: "Reader, I married him."). And for too many people, especially young women, alternative life paths are shut down, by themselves and society, almost before they have even been considered. While feminists of a certain stripe have spent years opposing marriage and trying to unseat marriage from its central place in the gendered imaginary, it is ironic to see marriage as an unquestioned good and a worthy goal in a gay imaginary. And it is not as if the opposition to marriage is a new thing and has gone unexpressed until now. Indeed, some of the earliest opposition to marriage came in the form of feminist critiques of what was then called "patriarchy." Feminists like Mary Wollstonecraft in the late eighteenth century in her *A Vindication of the Rights of Woman* described marriage as "legal prostitution." John Stuart Mill, some seventy years later, argued against marriage on the grounds that it coerced women to legally submit to unequal relations with men. Simone de Beauvoir, one hundred years later, reiterated Mill's point that marriage can never be freely chosen by women as long as it is based upon unequal relations between men and women, and she depicted marriage in *The Second Sex* as a trap for both sexes: however, while men can escape the confines of marriage through prostitution and the indulging of their "sexual caprices," women can only find a way out by cheating. Indeed, she writes: "Adultery becomes a natural part of marriage."[4] And it is this argument, that marriage necessitates adultery, that finds its way into contemporary feminist critiques of marriage by Laura Kipnis and others.

Laura Kipnis, in a hilarious and razor-sharp polemic, *Against Love,*[5] reveals how love lures young and unsuspecting idealists into marriage and then traps them there through a series of social set pieces that establish couples as each others' jailors (she gives the example of how couples have to tell each other everything they are doing, report back on where they are going and with whom, and check in periodically throughout the day or evening—recall the Lady Gaga video *Telephone* and the recurrent lyric "stop calling, stop calling"). Eventually one or both of the members of this "domestic gulag" rebels and escapes through an adulterous affair that offers a brief glimpse of freedom before it becomes love . . . and then marriage . . . and then the cycle begins again. In Kipnis's polemic, the social structure within which love occurs is the real problem, but because it is hard to change structural conditions, we instead blame each other for the dysfunction of love and marriage and agree to "work on it," going to therapy to do so. Kipnis's polemic is all the more effective for the way it nails some of the most familiar routines of married or even just coupled life, and so lets no one off the hook. The clichés of the wedding and romantic love, as she shows, quickly harden into the formulaic routines of married life; and so we tame, domesticate, and manage the explosive intimacies between lovers and turn them into the humdrum schedule of the everyday, leaving all the fantasy, the action, and the utopian possibility behind and dreaming of it only when we go to see the latest lame romantic comedy . . .

ONCE A BRIDESMAID . . .

So, to summarize: marriage is an agenda forced upon LGBT groups by the widespread opposition to gay marriage, and while some gays and lesbians choose to marry, it's not a cause that lies at the heart of queer community. Marriage flattens out the varied terrain of queer social life and reduces the differences that make queers, well, queer, to legal distinctions that can be ironed out by the strong hand of the law. Why not work on other forms of legal recognition than marriage, forms that allow for conventional and unusual household arrangements? Why invest only in long-term, permanent attachments? Why not think beyond marriage, especially at this moment when marriage is a floundering institution even for heterosexuals? In other words, how in the world did we end up with a gay agenda that seeks marriage equality when the world is going to hell in a handbag and what we really need is complete and utter social transformation?

Even Hollywood cinema and the popular press seem to know that marriage has exhausted its own fragile plot. In the last decade, actually mostly between 2008 and 2011, with 2009 being a banner year, Hollywood has produced a plethora of romantic comedies and bromances such as *Bride Wars* (2009), *Bridesmaids* (2011), *He's Just Not That Into You* (2009), *I Love You, Man* (2009), *The Hangover* (2009), *The Hangover Part II* (2011), *The*

Proposal (2009), *Forgetting Sarah Marshall* (2008), *Sex and the City* (2008), and *Sex and the City 2* (2010)—in which whiny women are desperate for love and marriage and randy men are desperate to escape both. In these films, women are either bitches or pathetic and men are either dopes or pathetic. After a vigorous critique of the whole marriage thing, these comedies all end with thoroughly unconvincing resolutions in anemic and barely believable weddings and romantic couplings. The entire premise of the movie versions of *Sex and the City*, for example, revolves around the very event marriage—that the TV series avoided in order to keep the four friends intact as a female unit of companionship. While the TV shows made the character of Carrie Bradshaw into a romantic single looking for love in all the wrong places, the movie begins when she has already met and moved in with Mr. Right, or Mr. Big, in this case. After years of defining herself in opposition to compulsory coupledom and in alliance with single womanhood, Carrie wants to get married, and she wants the wedding to be the biggest and the best ever. Well, predictably, the film depicts Mr. Big becoming increasingly nervous as the wedding gets more and more elaborate, and the more expensive and detailed the wedding becomes, the more Carrie wants and needs Mr. Big to want what she wants. When he finally calls it quits, she finally sees the error of her ways. When she finally comes to her senses, he finally agrees to the wedding she wants and needs. The film turns upon a critique of the superficial forms of romance that feed into the wedding industrial complex, and then it does an about-face and pays the piper, becoming, in spite of everything, a wedding.

The wedding is the "cum shot" of the romantic comedy. With its frothy white dresses, its ecstatic declarations of willingness ("I do, I do!"), its over-the-top cakes, and its abundance of clothing in unnatural materials, the wedding is the consummation of all the hopes and dreams that young women have been offered along the way to adulthood. The princesses, the pink toys, the unicorns (phallic symbol, anyone?), the romantic and impossible narrative of femininity will perhaps only ever be resolved by the charming, sometimes moving, often nauseating spectacle of the wedding. With their cookie-cutter plots, their beefcake leads, and their bimbo heroines, romantic comedies want only one thing—not the perfect love, the perfect partner, the perfect location, they want only a perfect wedding, and while in previous decades the romantic comedy (*When Harry Met Sally; Annie Hall; Moonstruck*) was about Mr. and Mrs. Right finding each other, now the genre dispenses altogether with the foreplay of finding each other and heads right to the wedding.

Take the plot of *Bridesmaids*, a recent rom-com, a film written by women (Kristen Wiig, who also stars in it, and Annie Mumolo) and starring a bevy of talented comic actresses. In *Bridesmaids*, the hapless heroine is single and out of work when her best friend announces that she is getting married. The plot now turns to the preparation for the wedding—the shower, the hen party, the wedding rehearsal. While the friends fight over who will be the maid of honor, the protagonist fails to notice that she has already met her own Mr. Right. Many critics, like Mary Elizabeth Williams at *Salon* (who called *Bridesmaids* "your first black president of female-driven comedies"),[6] were falling over themselves to announce this movie as a breakthrough for female-centered comedy, and feminist to boot. And, as A. O. Scott points out in his review of the film in the *New York Times*: "The men in the movie are kind of beside the point," and the real action is girl on girl.[7] As another critic, Michelle Dean at *The Awl*, reminded us, though, this was hardly a feminist breakthrough—99 percent of the discussions between women focused on marriage, family, and weddings![8] And in this film, the rom-com comes as close to a porno flick as it is possible to come without naked unconvincing sex to 1980s music. In other words, the men were just excuses for women to strut their stuff; the women perform sexy femininity with one another while men look on and while the female bodies are exposed, examined, and abused—the most obvious example of this laying bare of the female body can be seen in the movie's central gross-out scene, which plays with the tropes of disordered female embodiment in general and focuses therefore on food, on binging and purging, through a kind of involuntary bulimia. And so, following an ill-advised dinner (at a decidedly ethnic restaurant) for their hen night, the bridesmaids head for a dress fitting and, in the pristine chamber of virginal white gowns, they, one by one, throw up and shit uncontrollably in the grips of mass food poisoning. As Michelle Dean noted astutely, rather than making comedy out of the hideousness of bridal wear, the movie instead makes the women and not the clothes the place of horror.

In general, the women in rom-coms tend to come in about four varieties—the ones we see in *Sex and the City*, in fact:

1. *The Shrew* (Carrie) The shrew is often also the bride-to-be or, in mother-in-law films, represents the potential future of the spinster if she doesn't look out. If the shrew is young, then she is waiting to be tamed by the right man; if she is old, she is a cautionary figure.

2. *The Maid (of Honor)* (Charlotte) The maid is the unmarried friend of the bride, who represents the potential spinster in the making. She is the woman who makes bad choices, cannot keep a man, is abused by her boyfriends, and must be reformed over the course of the film into the next bride—the plot literally tries to throw her a bouquet.

3. *The Ugly Chick* (Miranda) The ugly chick is beyond marriage. She is the dyke, the fat one, the unmarriageable woman

who can be funny, nay, must be funny, because she is not pretty. She is, by implication, a lesbian; she is a professional woman too busy for a man, too oriented to her career, and so she has been diverted from her mission as a woman: to marry! In *Bridesmaids*, this is the Megan character played by Melissa McCarthy and the object of many "fat" and "ugly" jokes.

4. *The Other Woman* (Samantha) Every rom-com has an "other woman"—it might be the ex-girlfriend, the mother-in-law, the slutty rival, the high school friend who continues to haunt the protagonist. Her function is to push the bride to seal the deal with her guy.

Making the wedding into the money shot of the rom-com means raising and then overturning all objections to marriage in order to make the wedding meaningful, hard won, and a triumph. In *The Hangover*, the bromance prequel to *Bridesmaids*, we get the male perspective on all of this foreplay to marriage: while the girl version is a hen party gone horribly wrong, complete with female competition, eating-disorder activity—purging and binging—bitchiness, and an obligatory fat/ugly girl takedown, the boy version paints marriage as a bleak and bitter pill that the guy with full knowledge just has to man up to and swallow. The stag-party premise allows the guys to trash women, wives, and marriage while bonding with each other, beating up fags, and ogling strippers. In the case of *The Hangover*, we are given four men, the archetypal male players in the marriage tragedy:

1. *The Best Man* (Phil, played by Bradley Cooper) This is the stud who was gonna be somebody, who is all macho daring and yet who has been castrated by marriage and children and needs to get his mojo back by hanging out with his buddies.

2. *The Henpecked Husband or Husband-to-Be* (Stu, played by Ed Helms, who repeats this role in several other movies; *Cedar Rapids,* for example) This is the nice guy who tries too hard to please his passive-aggressive girlfriend and who has learned to bend his needs around hers and who needs to be liberated from her abuse by his buddies.

3. *The Loser* (Alan, played by Zach Galifianakis, who repeats this role ad nauseum in every movie he is in—see *Due Date* for example; Jonah Hill plays similar characters) This is the fat/hairy/hopeless guy, the romantic lead's unwanted friend/ brother-in-law who strikes out with women because he is a sociopath. As such he draws negative attention away from some of the hateful behavior of the other dudes and makes it seem like they are cool and sane because he is warped and mad. Despite being physically repulsive, he can sometimes get the girl and slip into the bridegroom-to-be role (see *Knocked Up*).

4. *The Bridegroom-to-Be* (Doug, played by Justin Bartha) He is a cipher, an excuse for a plot, the narrative equivalent of the penis rather than the phallus (a phallus is an idealized version of the penis, it is the power represented by the penis in a male-dominated society; or more succinctly, a phallus is a penis, only smaller . . .), and he is just the cork bobbing along on the waters of heterosexuality who becomes the target of his friends' attempts to rescue themselves from the deep waters of marriage by warning him against diving in.

These archetypes of the rom-com, male and female, are to be found in most specimens from the genre. Think of *He's Just Not That Into You*—the maid yearns for a guy of her own, the best man struggles with infidelity with the other woman, the shrew cannot reform and her husband leaves her, and the henpecked husband, the Ben Affleck character, transforms into the bridegroom by standing up to his wife-to-be. Or think of *The Proposal*—the Sandra Bullock character plays the shrew, who gets tamed by the henpecked husband-to-be (her assistant), who moves into the role of bridegroom by standing up to the shrew. Think of *Bridesmaids*—Kristen Wiig plays Annie, the maid; her best friend, Lillian (Maya Rudolph), is the shrew who finally gets her man, and Melissa McCarthy plays Megan, the ugly chick who comes on to every man and threatens to come on to the women, too. And Rose Byrne plays Helen, the classic other woman, who in this case is married but competes with Annie for the affections of Lillian. Having dispensed with the part of the plot where boy meets girl (boy is just there in this film, a cipher), the drama of the film is about friendship, horizontal relations among the bridesmaids rather than hierarchical relations between the couple and everyone else. While the film seems to offer something new by focusing upon the women and answering the stag bromances, it cleaves tightly to the three-act structure, the four archetypal characters, and the demand that the romantic comedy deliver all of its riotous sexual energy to the prison house of love and marriage.

While the screenplay writers get rich by feeding this shit into a machine and turning out one bad script after another, the marriage myth grows while the divorce rate rockets upward. Hell, we could all write these scripts in our spare time: woman works for guy in his office (or vice versa for something quirky); neither of them realize that they are in love, and they both get involved with other people but realize the mistake when (a) they all take a trip together, (b) they have to pretend to be together for some family function, or (c) they are forced to do something difficult together. Or, guy's friend gets married, he meets a woman at the wedding, loses her, finds her again as she is about to get married, intervenes . . . or, guy never wanted to get married, girl never wanted to settle down—guy and girl date casually and, wow, they fall for each other while doing all this casual-sex stuff. They resist each other, break up, nearly get back together again but don't and then do. Or, girl and guy accidentally get married while drunk and then try to get divorced, but just as the divorce comes through they realize—gasp—they really love each other.

Formulas can be sexy and fun, though, and it's not the formulaic quality of these romantic comedies that is the main problem—it is the critique of marriage that they raise (generically important because they have to put something in the way of marriage in order to romantically overcome the obstacle later) only to bury it later. As Gigi in *He's Just Not That Into You* (the central film in the female-punishment version of the rom-com) says in a nice speech right before she caves in to a dude who has treated her like shit:

> Every movie we see, every story we're told implores us to wait for it: the third act twist, the unexpected declaration of love, the exception to the rule. But sometimes we're so focused on finding our happy ending we don't learn how to read the signs, how to tell the ones who want us from the ones who don't, the ones who will stay and the ones who will leave. And maybe a happy ending doesn't include a guy, maybe it's you, on your own, picking up the pieces and starting over, freeing yourself up for something better in the future. Maybe the happy ending is just moving on.

Wow, great concept, maybe the happy ending *is* just moving on . . . but Gigi does not move on, and maybe no Hollywood-authored movie will provide such a happy ending because, just as the "happy ending" in porn is male orgasm, so the happy ending in the romantic comedy is female orgasm symbolized by the wedding. And so it goes: the institution of marriage stands naked and revealed, replete with all of its disappointments and coercive aspects, and yes, despite everything, the bridesmaid dreams of being a bride, the bridegroom makes a stand and then falls in line, and gays and lesbians march in the streets for the right to enter into the mayhem and mishap of holy matrimony.

WHITE WEDDINGS?

Is the wedding always white? In other words, is this narrative of male reluctance, desperate-housewives-to-be, and female pathos a story about white people or does it have a more universal application? Of course, the nasty little secret behind most romantic comedies is that the union of a man and a woman is only romantic if it meets certain expectations around race and class: and so, a rich white man can marry a white working woman (*Pretty Woman; Bridget Jones's Diary*) because this is a beloved fairy tale of the culture (*Cinderella*). It works less well if the guy is poor and the woman is rich, although this narrative also gets some mileage as long as (a) the newly minted couple are doomed (*Titanic*) or on a desert island (*Swept Away*). Films where black men are paired with white women are extremely rare, and even Denzel Washington, Will Smith, and Samuel L. Jackson are almost never cast against white heroines. When they are, as in the 1999 film *The Bone Collector,* which starred Denzel Washington and Angelina Jolie, the chance of an actual sexual relationship is as limited as Denzel's character's mobility—he is confined to a wheelchair. In *Hitch,* Will Smith plays a love doctor to a white guy, and his own romantic possibility comes in the form of Eva Mendez, not a white woman. The combinations of bodies that are seen as "romantic" in Hollywood must not violate certain notions of racial mixing or sexual fetishism; the plot lines try to push race firmly to one side, and if the love story does feature people of color then it is mostly about people of color romancing other people of color. While in *Bridesmaids* the bride is actually black, the cultural differences between her family and her spouse-to-be's are never raised, and the only real sign of those differences takes the form of a jazz band at the engagement party.

In black films where the wedding becomes the central force of the narrative, films like Salim Akil's *Jumping the Broom* (2011), we find many of the conventional tropes about uppity women and deadbeat guys, but there is often a class narrative that creates a warring-families scenario, with the "ghetto" family creating problems by behaving resentfully and having meltdowns and the wealthy black family creating other problems by being snooty and emotionally repressed. In *Jumping the Broom* the groom's badly behaved postal-worker mother stands off against the bride's badly behaved trust-fund-endowed Caribbean mother. The fathers are absent (dead) or feminized (worse than dead), and while the bride has to make herself pure and worthy of love, the groom has to learn lessons in manhood and become worthy of fatherhood. Formulaic as the black wedding films may be (*Why Did I Get Married?* and *Why Did I Get Married Too?* directed by Tyler Perry, also fall in this category and even feature some of the same actors), they are at least dealing with more than just the anxiety of landing a man. They address head-on the struggles with long-term commitment, the historically negative representations of the black family, and the looming issue of racism.

Jumping the Broom tries to expand the limitations of the genre by making the African American couple-to-be a jetsetter match who are on their way to China (a symbol of global prosperity and new labor markets), and by confronting a new future for black reproductive politics without abandoning the past (slavery as symbolized by the broom itself). But ultimately, this film and others like it that focus on black marriage politics, tie black futurity securely to heterosexuality, respectability, and a bootstrap politics of aspiration. They teem with anxieties about black manhood; they worry about black matriarchs who are suffocating their sons, about aggressive women who will smother their husbands, and about uppity daughters who will abandon the black family altogether. These films are less worried, in other words, about marriage per se and more concerned with the survival of the black family and, by extension, the black community.

Other films that contest the "white wedding" romance include the small but significant genre of Asian American marriage movies, South Asian as well as Southeast Asian, and these films, like *Monsoon Wedding* (2001, directed by Mira Nair), *The Wedding Banquet* (1993, directed by Ang Lee), and *The Joy Luck Club* (1993, directed by Wayne Wang), focus pretty closely on the clashes between generations that are so much a part of conventional immigrant narratives, and the tension between so-called traditional ways (including arranged marriages) and modern modes of romance. They often feature gay characters and plots, as if to equate modernity with homosexuality and diaspora with sexual tolerance.

Basically, the wedding plots that are so much a part of the contemporary politics of marriage confirm the instability of the institution at the very moment that gays and lesbians are knocking at the door. Indeed, so hackneyed is the genre that a recent film, *Friends with Benefits* (2011, directed by Will Gluck), actually parodied the formulaic quality of the romance film and had the characters spout the rules of the game as if they were about to break them . . . of course, this self-consciousness did not prevent them from falling in love and living happily ever after. And there's the rub! We may all know, see, and acknowledge the clichéd quality of the romance plot, but until we are raised with different understandings of love, desire, and intimacy, we must still cleave to it, still long for the happily ever after, and still find ourselves disappointed and devastated, stranded at the altar like a jilted bride who believed that marriage would make her happy but discovered that, like the wedding, marriage is overpriced, overvalued, overestimated, and maybe soon, simply over.

GAGA POLITICS

I want to end this chapter by making an argument for a more quirky politics, a gaga politics made up of a fanciful agenda less oriented toward legal inclusion and more oriented to a queer project of reimagining life worlds by understanding the history of the present—or how the hell we came to this particular arrangement of bodies in space and time, this understanding of relation and separation, attachment and commitment, this orientation to property and money. Antimarriage queer activists have not settled for simply offering a critique. There is much that is visionary in the insights they provide. Trans activist Dean Spade, for example, works on administrative law, and he argues that the gay and lesbian organizations that advocate for access to "the security and entitlements distributed by regulatory state institutions" are misguided, because in so doing they "fail to oppose the very mechanisms that maintain and reproduce inequality." Spade and his collaborator Craig Willse see gay marriage as primarily an issue for "racially and economically privileged lesbians and gay men," and they push for "alternative modes of resisting the coercive state regulation of sexuality, gender and family structure."[9] These include fighting on behalf of much broader social projects with benefits for a much wider swath of the population, and abandoning identity politics in favor of joining forces with the "struggles of those who experience the greatest impact" of state-authorized and -issued inequality and discrimination. Spade even has a chart that counters every argument made for marriage with an alternative argument and an alternative plan of action.

Contemporary feminist visionaries also offer other ways of thinking and being in relation to marriage, capital, and the status quo. J. K. Gibson-Graham is the pen name of a visionary duo of feminist political theorists, the late Julie Graham and Katherine Gibson, who argue for "the end of Capitalism as we knew it." Their main political strategy involves seeing alternatives to the status quo, particularly alternatives to capitalism and neoliberal economic programs and working in the spaces in between normative constructions of labor, worth, kinship, and intimacy. In their work, they argue that we are so convinced that capitalism as an economic system is invincible, that we actually stop seeing all the ways in which we engage already in noncapitalist modes of exchange. Swap meets, co-ops, neighborly exchanges of labor and goods are all examples of informal economic systems that stand outside of profit-oriented systems.

Teaching us to learn to see the alternatives that surround us, Gibson-Graham perform a great pedagogical act. If we apply it to the question of marriage, we might find that while marriage seems inevitable as a social form, in fact we all know people who not only do not get married but are happily single or polyamorous or live in threesomes. On a recent trip to Mexico City, for example, I met a couple, two women, who seemed comfortably ensconced in a long-term relationship. But when we met up later in the day with a third person, a friend of theirs, I became confused about who was with whom. I could see multiple intimacies, and the streamlined inevitability of the couple form suddenly became overgrown with the complications of other connections and desires. Finally, curious, I asked about who was actually living with whom, and I discovered that the women were a long-term threesome and had been living together as a trio for over a decade. Two of the women had been together for much longer, but they had incorporated the third partner a decade earlier. While it was hard for me to understand how the arrangement worked, I felt as if I was in the presence of something very different, an intimate arrangement that never did lapse into the same kinds of rhythms that a coupled relationship might and that had its own logic, complications, pleasures, and trajectories embedded within it. As Gibson-Graham points out, it is not that other ways of being do not exist, it is that we lack the imagination to see and comprehend them.

For some thinkers, challenging the inevitability of certain social forms, like the couple, say, can lead us to take issue with other seemingly obvious connections. Take for example the connections we assume to exist between rights and freedom; inclusion and progress; access and equality. In an essay titled "Gestural Critique of Judgment," visionary scholar Fred Moten argues for the *right to refuse rights*.[10] Moten ties Joan Dayan's question in relation to Guantanamo Bay prisoners: "What does it mean to have lost the right to have rights?" to an earlier, postcolonial question by theorist Gayatri Spivak, namely: "Can the Subaltern Speak?" While Dayan's question about prisoners names a place outside the law where prisoners have not only been placed at odds with the law but seem to have lost access to legality altogether, Spivak's question about whether the disenfranchised can speak really questions whether privileged people can actually hear what those they have trampled upon have to say. Especially when what someone has to say comes in a form other than the clichéd language of freedom and rebellion. And so, asking, "What does it mean to have the right to refuse the rights that have been refused to you?" Moten continues: "What does it mean to be against or outside of the law of the home and the state, the home and the state that you constitute and which refuses you? What does it mean to refuse that which has been refused you? What new infusion is made possible by such refusal?"[11]

Moten shows us how to see the political landscape in ways that are not already determined by preexisting forms but that wrestle with the possibility that some people may want to live and die outside of state forms of regulation, governance, and rescue. Moten's call here for the right of refusal could be deployed to refuse the battle for the right to marry, to refuse the presumed connection between marriage rights and liberation, to refuse to succumb to the idea that coupled monogamy is now and has always been the best and most stable way to practice intimacy. To refuse to ask for the rights that have been refused to you is to turn your back on the carrot dangled by the state and to go looking for nourishment elsewhere.

And if these intellectual guides are not enough or do not appeal, I give you, again, Dory from *Finding Nemo*. Voiced by the effervescent Ellen DeGeneres, Dory is a great model for future quirky politics. Dory, as discussed in chapter 3, is the forgetful fish who can only remember things for five minutes at a time and then has to begin again. Her disability notwithstanding, Dory is able to find the missing Nemo, navigate the way across the Pacific, speak whale, and lead a fish uprising against fishermen. She accomplishes all of this, I might add, while remaining firmly outside the nuclear triangle that she and Nemo's father, Marlon, and Nemo seem fated to form. Indeed, she is a marriage resister who, in rebuffing the seemingly inevitable narrative conclusion of romantic marriage to Marlon and parenthood to Nemo, finds common cause with many other kinds of creatures and unites with them against the biggest threat to their shared future: man, capitalism, and ecological collapse. She literally forgets family, forgets to get married, forgets to become a mother, and in the process opens herself up to a new way of being. I suggest we do the same.

FIVE

Gaga Manifesto

*No party or government, no army, school or institution will
ever emancipate a single person.*

—Jacques Rancière, *The Ignorant Schoolmaster*

*It cannot be denied that the university is a place of refuge,
and it cannot be accepted that the university is a place of
enlightenment. In the face of these conditions one can only
sneak into the university and steal what one can. To abuse
its hospitality, to spite its mission, to join its refugee colony,
its gypsy encampment, to be in but not of—this is the path
of the subversive intellectual in the modern university.*

—Fred Moten and Stefano Harney,
"The University and the Undercommons"

It's all in the game, yo.

—Omar in *The Wire*

The manifesto, from Karl Marx to Valerie Solanas, has played
with utopian possibility while also proposing a plan of action.
For Marx, the plan was for the workers of the world to rise
up and take action against those who profit from their labor;
for Solanas, the manifesto was a modest proposal, a contract
with future generations of women whom she would save from
the inequities of patriarchy by "cutting up men." For the futur-
ists, an early-nineteenth-century art movement based in Italy,
the manifesto voiced a break with the past, a definitive refusal
to be bound to tradition and weighed down by history and

expectation. And in Lady Gaga's 2011 video *Born This Way*, the "Monster Mother's Manifesto" is some weird sci-fi shit about choosing good over evil after emerging from an egg covered in goo! Most manifestos combine the radical and the reactionary, the reasonable and the preposterous, hard cold analysis with fantastical visions. I am using my Gaga Manifesto to push us further into the crisis, into the eye of the hurricane, deep into the heart of nonsense. And so . . . to continue:

IN A CRISIS, IN THIS CRISIS, DON'T REMAIN CALM . . . GET AGITATED AND ADD TO THE CHAOS.

> *Organizations are obstacles to organizing ourselves.*
> —The Invisible Committee

Welcome to the gagapocalypse! As the environmental crisis turns from bad to worse, as wars break out like wildfire across the globe, as bankers and corporate gamblers take higher and higher shares of the global markets, and as the social rituals that formerly held communities together lose their meaning, it is time to go gaga. In a crisis, do not remain calm, do not look for the nearest exit, do not stick your head in the sand; do agitate, do make things worse, do run screaming through the street, and do refuse to return to business as usual.

Business as usual is what created this mess in the first place. Business as usual has meant that businesspeople and corporate fat cats run/ruin the world and artists are out of luck; it has meant that education, spirituality, sexuality all must function on a business model and every attempt to make changes is greeted with a pragmatic question about whether changing things will also mean making money. Making money cannot be the goal of the new feminism. Putting women in positions of power is not what gaga feminism wants. What gaga feminism wants cannot be easily summarized, but it is not an independent bank account, not a profitable nonprofit; mama does not want a brand new bag. Mama wants revolution, but gaga revolution may not be one that Karl Marx or Valerie Solanas would recognize.

And as we have seen in the 2011 riots, protests, and occupations happening around the world, especially in urban centers, we seem to have entered a new era of anticorporate and anticolonial struggle in which the form matters as much as the content. No longer satisfied with simply marching or issuing a list of demands, these new movements turn politics into performance and combine anarchist mistrust of structure with queer notions of bodily riot and antinormative disruption.

The markers of this new form of politics, in addition to the lack of a clear agenda or list of demands and the strong presence of a clear belief in the rightness of the cause, display an unusual mix of whimsy and fierce purposefulness, ludic improvisation and staying power, passive resistance and loud refusals. The occupations recognize that in an economy that engineers success for an elite few at the expense of the failure of the many, failure becomes a location for resisting, blocking, slowing, jamming the economy and the social stability that depends upon it. So, in a world where 1 percent of the population benefits from the ruin of the other 99 percent, we might want to think about failure as what Professor James C. Scott calls one of the "weapons of the weak."[1] Scott draws attention to the multiple ways in which radically disempowered people have exerted their own forms of resistance through actions and inactions that can be overlooked or misread but that constitute an elaborate web of subversive gestures. Foot-dragging, feigned incompetence, stupidity, and laziness are all cast as the features of a people who cannot rule themselves and so must be ruled, but can actually be understood better as a commitment to refuse the logic of rule—be it colonial, capitalist, feudal, or neoliberal. And while there are clear and important differences between the forms of power in each system—be it power exercised bureaucratically or financially, violently or hegemonically—there are always places where the most dispersed systems of power manifest as unadulterated violence and where the most forceful modes of resistance become more creative, surreptitious, or more cunning.

The 99 percents in many ways use the language of colonialism—occupation—and the techniques of anticolonial struggle—refusal and mimicry. They also circumvent certain logics of power that would dictate the terms of resistance and engage in activities that are hard to read as action at all. They don't want to present a manifesto, they actually are themselves the manifestation of discontent. The 99 percenters simply show up, take up space, make noise, witness. This is a form of political response that doesn't announce itself as politics; instead, it enters quietly into the public sphere, sits down, and refuses to leave. Insightful commentators such as Harsha Walia have pointed out that to some indigenous peoples, the occupation movements sound a rhetoric of territorialization that is all too familiar, and so Walia suggests that the movements need to acknowledge that they are occupying already occupied lands, lands that were already peopled by native groups and that settler colonialists claimed in the land grabs of the nineteenth century. Walia gives as examples the Hudson Bay Company in Canada and the East India Company in India, both of which were corporate interests that exploited land and people in the colonial period.[2] But Walia goes on to acknowledge the power of these movements and explains that their power lies in their ability to be "transitional" and to eschew individual rights projects in favor of the broad goal of imagining another kind of world. Walia also cites influential philosopher Slavoj Zizek, who addressed Occupy Wall Street protestors and warned the crowd of the danger of co-optation. Zizek cautioned: "The problem is that the system pushes you to give up. Beware not only of the enemies. But also of false friends who are already working to dilute this process . . . They will try to make this into a harmless moral protest."[3]

Here I depart from Walia and feel compelled to name Zizek as potentially one of the co-optors himself, in that he always anticipates co-optation and often even helps it along. Zizek denounced the London riots in an article titled "Shoplifters of the World Unite,"[4] making it seem as if the rioters were just mall-rats on a consumer rampage. When he addressed the OWS crowd, he commented: "Carnivals come cheap. What matters is the day after, when we will have to return to normal life. Will there be any changes then? I don't want you to remember these days you know, like 'oh, we were young, it was beautiful.' Remember that our basic message is 'We are allowed to think about alternatives.'" True indeed that the basic message is that there are always alternatives, but the idea that "carnivals come cheap" misses the point of the entire occupy movement. This *is* a carnival, and carnivals are precisely protests, and they are protests that never envision a return to "normal life" but see normal life as one of the fictions of colonial and neocolonial power, a fiction used to bludgeon the unruly back into resignation. Like many anticolonial and anticapitalist movements, this current movement refuses to envision an outcome, eschews utopian or pragmatic conjurings of what happens on the "morning after," precisely because the outcome will be decided upon by the process of dissent, refusal, and carnivalesque failure. All we can know for sure is that the protests signal and announce a collective awareness of the end of "normal life."

In Glenn Beck's favorite book to hate of the last few years, *The Coming Insurrection*, the Invisible Committee, an anonymous group of French anarchists, write on behalf of their manifesto: "Everyone agrees. It's about to explode." They go on to urge that we exploit the current economic crisis by blocking the economy; that we build upon the ruins of the social by reimagining relation within a "wild and massive experimentation with new arrangements and fidelities"; and that we "organize beyond and against work."[5] The book is a kind of contemporary Situationist manifesto: like the Situationists, a revolutionary group also founded in France, in 1957, the Invisible Committee strives to use art and social disruption to exploit economic crisis and bring about the collapse of capitalism. The Invisible Committee, like the Situationists, believe that people need to be woken from their slumber by public actions, odd and eclectic events that shock and inspire people and compel us all to look for alternatives to the status quo. *The Coming Insurrection* is inspired in its logic and uncanny in its timing (given the recent insurrections around the globe, from Europe to the Middle East), and it unites fragments from queer theory ("the future has no future") and punk DIY ethics ("make the most of every crisis") with feminist insights about the implication of the family in the "great social debacle" that we called economic prosperity ("everyone feels the inanity of the sad family nucleus"). Rarely are such insights brought together on a revolutionary platform.

The Invisible Committee, unlike other anarchist projects, does not just imagine a world free of state power, it follows the thread of that concept through other organizational units that stand in for the state. And so, queer anarchism would extend the critique of institutions to the family. While many anarchist thinkers—people like Pierre-Joseph Proudhon and Peter Kropotkin, Emma Goldman and Guy Debord—believed in free love or polyamory, and while some (Goldman was one) issued stinging critiques of marriage, most have paid less attention to sex, love, and the family and more to economic exchange, questions of violence and revolution. But, as the Invisible Committee makes very clear, there can be no viable concept of revolt today that does not link the personal and political, the private and the public, the particular and the general. There can be no sidelining of feminism, queer politics, questions of intimacy and kinship.

Gaga feminism leads the way to an anarchist project of cultural riot and reciprocation: what Kropotkin called "mutual aid,"[6] the tendency for animals to cooperate rather than compete (in the way that Darwin presumed all species competed for survival), becomes today a newly vital model for human interaction. Mutual aid or mutual protection or new notions of exchange actually flourish already in the worlds we inhabit and those we are making as we go—open-source exchanges on the Web, cooperative food collectives, subcultures, new modes of kinship, and different understandings of our mutual responsibilities exist already for the purpose of exchange and not profit, and this notion of working with others rather than in competition is probably the only thing that will save us from the greed of free-market economies.

And it is this gaga spirit of anarchy that I believe courses through Lady Gaga's music and forms the spine of a liberatory anthem. Forget about "Born This Way" and focus on the rhythmic freefall accomplished by Lady Gaga, especially in her live performances. Lady Gaga's music may not itself stray far from pop, but when she performs it in crazy costumes and with wild abandon, we have a sense of the new world that she opens up, for young people in particular. In recent years she has performed with a number of different artists who make up a kind of compressed history of gaga feminism: Yoko Ono, for example. Yoko Ono's 2009 album, *Between My Head and the Sky*, features a collection of rather spunky songs with dark themes but a bouncy,

new-wave treatment. From the track "The Sun Is Down" to the final cut, a short statement set to a sparse percussion—"It's Me, I'm
Alive," the seventy-six-year-old icon yelps, howls, and chants her
way through a multigenre journey to the dark side. But, in Ono's
wild duet with Lady Gaga from their live show together at the
Orpheum in Los Angeles in 2010, captured by a fan and posted to
YouTube, the point is not to mourn a life passed or an opportunity
missed or the end of light. Ono and Gaga instead ride a cacopho-
nous tide into a funky frenzy when they howl their way through
"The Sun Is Down." The two join forces for this dark duet, dark
both in terms of its theme and in the refusal of the forward mo-
mentum of the pop song, and they push each other to new levels
of going gaga. The short video clip on YouTube presents a very
different Gaga, a very different Ono. But the duet also crafts a
family resemblance between Gaga and Ono and emphasizes the
dark streak that resonates through Ono's performance history.
Ono, of course, has had a long career of performance art marked
by masochistic presentations like *Cut Piece*, where she allows the
audience to cut off her clothes, or *Painting to Be Stepped On*, in
which the audience marks up and in a way destroys her canvas,
or *Hide and Seek Piece*, about which she wrote this in her book
Grapefruit: "Hide until everybody goes home. Hide until everybody forgets about you. Hide until everybody dies."[7] Ono's work
with Gaga sits comfortably alongside her early jazz work with
Ornette Coleman and John Cage, which is filled with screaming
and vocal noise. But in performing this piece as a duet with Lady
Gaga, Ono's corpus, filled as it is with dark noise, circles of repeti-
tion, a resistance to sense making, speaks anew, and Lady Gaga's
media-friendly, pop-heavy orientation is quickly contaminated by
the noisy riot of going gaga.

Lady Gaga does not emerge from a vacuum, nor does she
spring fully formed in the space vacated by Madonna, Gwen

Stefani, and Britney Spears. She is in fact the last manifestation
of a long line of feminine and queer performers who have used
their time in the spotlight to produce funky forms of anarchy,
to demonstrate an antisentimental fascination with loss, lack,
darkness, and wild performance and to dig into the intersections
of punk and glamour to find songs of madness and mayhem.
While most commentators on the Gaga phenomenon are content to trace Lady Gaga's lineage back through her time at NYU
and her connections to other blond performers, the real story is
much richer—Gaga, according to an interview she gave in 2011
to fashion designer Jean Paul Gaultier, first started calling herself
Lady Gaga after meeting Lady Starlight, a self-proclaimed scene
queen and party promoter. Lady Starlight reportedly told Lady
Gaga that she was doing something much more than making
music, she was, said Lady Starlight, making art. Lady Starlight
was quite right. Gaga goes beyond the pop songs and becomes
art. This makes Lady Gaga part of a very different group of
performers. Thus, instead of tethering her to pop hopefuls who
came before her, we need to make the connections to a long
line of feminine anarchists, musicians, and writers, people like
Emma Goldman but also Grace Jones, Shulamith Firestone but
also Yoko Ono, Marina Abramovic but also Ari Up of the Slits
or Poly Styrene of X-Ray Spex. As Lady Gaga herself has said:
"I mean not to be so direct but I just think that people need to
come up with better references than Christina and Gwen and
Madonna all the time."[8]

Lady Gaga might be engaged in the same kind of project as
the Invisible Committee. While they encourage people to "find
each other" and start making different forms of connection, Lady
Gaga coolly dissects the pop market and finds new sounds, new
messages, and new forms of political engagement. She tweets,
she texts, she uses every medium available; she sings about the

phone and indeed becomes a phone. She knows about the Coming Insurrection because it partly takes the form of Gaga herself.

The Invisible Committee also implicates university systems in the production of false hierarchies motored by people "who always ask permission before taking. Who silently respect culture, the rules, and those with the best grades. Even their attachment to their great critical intellectuals," they write, "and their rejection of capitalism are stamped by this love of school."

I love this little book; it speaks to me and about me, calling to me in a way that much academic work does not. I like that it has no "author," that it refuses grand narratives, and that it proceeds without the endless academic quarrels that drag down even the most inspired critical attempts to make bold interventions. The book engages some genres that we do not traffic in enough as professors and as people who speak and write for a living—namely, manifestos, bold predictions, calls to arms—and it also names some important truths about failing economies, failing family structures, elitist universities, and the opportunities that arise out of the ashes of an older form of politics as such. The book pulls together the strings of social upheaval and catches a slice of revolution in its net. "Everyone agrees," they write. "It's about to explode"—in Cairo, in Ramallah, in Athens, in Los Angeles, the insurrection is coming and the Invisible Committee urges us to "find each other" soon. It also reminds us that true anarchy is not the absence of all modes of organization; indeed, effective anarchy requires that the ground be cleared first. But what creative anarchy does insist upon is that we organize separate from organizations, because "organizations are an obstacle to organizing ourselves." Creative anarchy, gaga anarchy, gaga feminism are all born of a spirit of experimentation, cooperation, change, motility, combustibility, and urgency. Seek intellectual emancipation in new modes of communication and

new forms of social relation. Failing that, clog the machinery
that manufactures the new by simply repackaging the old.

Gaga feminism advocates for being the fly in the ointment,
the wrench in the machinery, the obstacle to the smooth, the
seamless, and the quiet extension of the status quo. To go gaga is
to be loud in a world of silent collaborators, to be crazy in a room
full of nice and normal people, to be unpredictable in a world of
highly structured systems of meaning. But being gaga is not a
mindless commitment to some neoliberal concept of difference
and uniqueness. It is not another version of the sad, worn-out
notion of human diversity. It does not sacrifice the whole for the
part, the group for the individual, the multitude for the singular.
Of course, we are all trained to write liberation in the tired language of human uniqueness, but while millions of people allow
a deep-seated belief that everyone is different to legitimize their
absolute investments in political uniformity, gaga feminists want
to uncover bigger political prizes than splendid individualism.

As I was trying to sort through how and why it is that North
Americans in particular continue to invest political hope in the
chimera of individualism, I was listening to a Fleet Foxes song
titled "Helplessness Blues." The song first struck me as impossibly saccharine, hopelessly sentimental and needlessly shiny and
good. But as you listen, the song pulls out of its peppy tune and
descends into a grander and darker mood, and a different narrative emerges. The lyric begins as follows:

I was raised up believin'
I was somehow unique
like a snowflake, distinct among snowflakes
unique in each way you can see

Well, that was what got me at first—the old snowflakes analogy that appeals so much to those spreading the ideology of

individualism. Hey, by the way, cancer is also defined in terms of its uniqueness, but we rarely hear that analogy used to figure human diversity! As the author of the Pulitzer Prize–winning biography of cancer, *The Emperor of All Maladies*, Siddhartha Mukherjee puts it: "Normal cells are identically normal; malignant cells become unhappily malignant in unique ways."[9] To me this is actually a far better description of uniqueness—what is unique to each human is not the normal but the mutation; either you value mutation and uniqueness or you invest in the normal and the lack of difference. To stretch the analogy even further, either you want uniqueness and therefore you deliberately deviate from the norm or you want conformity and you settle for being just like everyone else. And it is no accident that those brave souls who do choose mutation and deviance over stasis and obedience are often represented as a plague on society. But generally speaking, Americans want to have it both ways—they want to be unique and normal at the same time—uniquely normal! Sorry folks, it is one or the other, and each opens onto reactionary and revolutionary possibilities.

Back to the song then. Fleet Foxes dump the snowflake analogy quickly; almost as quickly as you recognize it and sneer at it, it is gone, and the alternative folk band sing:

And now after some thinkin'
I'd say I'd rather be
a functioning cog in some great machinery
serving something beyond me.
But I don't, I don't know what that will be.
I'll get back to you someday
Soon you will see.

In a compact poetic tribute to collectivity, Fleet Foxes put to rest the seductive definition of the human as unique, and then they float the idea of serving a higher cause than individualism, harking back to a notion that was romantic for earlier generations but that has faded from popularity as words like "socialism" have been beaten to a pulp in the age of global capitalism and the aftermath of Soviet misrule. Without needing to name the version of collectivity for which the song holds out hope ("I don't know what that will be"), the utopian impulse of the song lies in its desire to locate both the possibility and the naming of that possibility somewhere in the future. A gaga feminism does not need to know and name the political outcome of its efforts. More important is to identify the form that transformative struggle should take. In this book I have named these forms variously as: making peace with the anarchy of childishness, entering into new forms of relation and family, resisting the legitimizing structures of marriage and kinship, and finding creative spaces within which to go gaga and in the process catching a glimpse of the something else that we call the (queer) future.

And so, like Fleet Foxes, while we reject the comfy notion of human uniqueness, we celebrate variation, mutation, cooperation, transformation, deviance, perversion, and diversion. These modes of change, many of which carry negative connotations, actually name the way that people take the risks that are necessary to shove our inert social structures rudely into the path of the oncoming gagapocalypse. Making change means stepping off the beaten path, making detours around the usual, and distorting the everyday ideologies that go by the name of "truth" or "common sense." Gaga feminism is what Del LaGrace Volcano, the notorious and brilliant photographer of queer bodies, would call a "sublime mutation," a chance encounter between the desire for something new and the will to create it or to think it. In his book *Sublime Mutations*, a treatise on queer embodiments and the outrageous forms they sometimes take, LaGrace Volcano

provides gorgeous glossy photographs of bodies in transition—
from male to female, female to male, female to female, male to
who knows what . . . and so on.[10] Rather than simply providing
a window onto bodily difference for voyeurs, however, LaGrace
Volcano also highlights the new and complex attractions exerted
by these new bodies. A trans man with a hormonally enhanced
clitoris becomes, in LaGrace Volcano's lens, not a failed man
or a grotesque woman but a wild and new gender with different genitalia, representing new opportunities for eros in a world
saturated with explicit imagery.

A clue as to how to accomplish this mode of thinking that
bypasses the logic, the form, and the content of traditional
thought comes in the form of what Italian Marxist philosopher
Paolo Virno calls "virtuosity," and French iconoclast Jacques
Rancière calls "improvisation." While for Virno, virtuosity is
what happens when the speaker/singer/musician begins to ar-
ticulate without the benefit of a script, for Rancière, improvisation is a mode of breaking with the systems of recognition
that keep us locked into the properly academic values of com-
petence, legitimacy, and science.[11] Drawing from the example of
the eighteenth-century educator Joseph Jacotot, Rancière claims
that conventional, discipline-based pedagogy demands the presence of a master and schools students not to think critically but
only to respect the superior knowledge, training, and intellect of
the schoolmaster and to want to reproduce it. While the "good"
teacher leads his students through the pathways of rationality,
the "ignorant schoolmaster," Jacotot discovered, must actually
allow them to get lost in order for them to experience confusion
and then find their own way out or back or around. Intellectual
emancipation, then, stems from three principles for Jacotot: "All
people have equal intelligence; every man can instruct himself;
everything is in everything." As we go loudly and grandly gaga,

we should be aiming for nothing less than intellectual emancipation, nothing less than total transformation of learning, and nothing short of chaos. In order to disorder the university and to undo the hegemonic project of the university, we need to think small but act big, take risks, and propel ourselves into the path of all kinds of coming insurrections.

KNOW THE GAME, BE THE GAME, PLAY THE GAME, CHANGE THE GAME . . .

If you know where to look, you can find pieces of gaga feminism and gaga ideology strewn across alternative forms of popular culture. In the acclaimed HBO series *The Wire*, we find many life lessons and hard-knock truths about "the game" or the perpetual struggle between the law and those people it fails to protect, the street and those people who are sacrificed upon it, professions and those people who learn how to work their success while engineering everyone's else's failure. *The Wire*, set in Baltimore, in five glorious seasons, explores the warfare between drug dealers and drug addicts, between detectives and city hall, between the fine shades of right and the nuanced areas of wrong. And all of these epic, Shakespearian dramas play out against the backdrop of school, kinship, intimacy, homoerotic bonding, lesbian parenting, divorce, alcoholism, courage, love, and loss.

There are so many great examples in *The Wire* of how the game is rigged, rigged in favor of white people, rich people, middle-class people, straight people, that it is hard to pick just one. But if we look at the symbolism of chess that plays through the whole series, we can find a few of the great moral lessons in creative anarchy laid out here. In an early episode from season one, D'Angelo, the ill-fated nephew of drug kingpin Barksdale, tries to teach some of his street soldiers, the drug slingers, the function of the various pieces on the chessboard. "Now, the king,

he move one space any direction he damn choose, 'cause he's the
king. Like this, this, this, a'ight? But he ain't got no hustle. But
the rest of these motherfuckers on the team, they got his back.
And they run so deep, he really ain't gotta do shit."[12] One of
his buddies answers: "Like your uncle." Right, like D'Angelo's
uncle, the chess king moves very little, gets good protection, and
hides behind his army. The queen, however, who in *The Wire*
comes in the form of the Robin Hood gay character Omar, the
queen, says D'Angelo: "She smart, she fast. She move any way
she want, as far as she want. And she is the go-get-shit-done
piece." Like all queens, she will be sacrificed if necessary for
the good of the king, but in the meantime, she can wreak havoc
and mayhem. D'Angelo goes on to explain how the pawns live
on the frontlines but move forward all the time trying to get to
the promised land where they will become rich and protected
themselves. "So, how do you get to be king?" asks one enter-
prising pawn. D'Angelo answers: "It ain't like that. See, the king
stay the king, a'ight? Everything stay who he is. Except for the
pawns. Now, if the pawn make it all the way down to the other
dude's side, he get to be queen. And like I said, the queen ain't
no bitch. She got all the moves." D'Angelo disabuses his audience of the idea that they can win the game—they can convert to
queens, they can run wild, but more likely they will be gunned
down and "out of the game early." The king stays the king, the
queen lives in glory for short spells but has everyone gunning for
her, and the pawns are sacrificed along the way for bigger prizes.
And that's the game.

In *The Wire*, however, the game is not only played on the
streets, it is also what defines the police department, which has
its own kings, queens, and pawns, and in the final season, the
press becomes another chessboard, with journalists and editors
positioning themselves, ready to make hits, take hits, play the

game, leave the game. In the pressroom, a white guy, watched closely by his black editor, begins to make up stories, embellish the truth, invent quotes in pursuit of good copy. The black editor calls him out on it, but lacking support from higher up, his objections are smothered. In a regular TV show, the bad journalist, like the bad cop or even the bad drug dealer, would go down in a blaze of ignominy and the person who brings him down would triumph and bask in the glory of being right, exposing wrong, and having integrity.

But this is *The Wire*, and the king, or power systems, "stay the king." The renegade hustlers, the queens, have power, too, but their power is movement, oversight, knowledge—it is not necessarily the power to change the game. And so, in the pressroom, the king stays the king, the white guy who has fabricated the news wins a Pulitzer Prize; the Latina who writes true copy at the desk next to him gets punitively transferred to a small local paper; the black editor who could see through the fake stories, who knows right from wrong, truth from lies, gets demoted and watches the drama of rewards and privilege play out its sad script from a distance. The series ends on this note—kings stay kings, queens do damage and then get neutralized, pawns leave the game early, knights and bishops make the moves they make but ultimately stay in the middle of the board not moving up or down. And that's the game, the game by which we all live and die; while a few win, most lose, and ultimately the game plays us.

Gaga feminism recognizes that the world rewards the corrupt, the cheaters, and the liars, and that dishonesty pays. Therefore, the only way to advance toward total disruption of inertia and complacency is to steal from the rich, undermine the religious, and upset the moralists. You cannot win in a world where the game is fixed, so resign yourself to losing. Gaga feminism is for the failures, the losers, those for whom the price of success is too high and the effect of losing may even be to open more doors. Gaga feminism is the ideology that motivates the queen in the chess match—as the queen, you can make big moves, bold moves, aggressive moves. You can do damage, take others out, move at will. You will also have everyone gunning for you, coming for you, following you. You will go down. But, in the words of Lady Gaga: "Don't be a drag, just be a queen."

SURVIVE THE GAME . . .

So, what do we have so far? A coming insurrection, a little intellectual emancipation through improvisation, a break with conventional knowledge, and a map to gaga feminism that will most likely take us to the edge, to the abyss, to chaos, to a new understanding of anarchy and to the road to unlearning. This manifesto offers insurrections, emancipation, insurgent, irrational revelry. It also reminds us that we are not here to win, to conquer, to rule. Our goals are simple and modest—gaga feminism proposes to be a new kind of gender politics for a new generation, a generation less bound to the romance of permanence (in the form of marriage, for example), more committed to the potential of flexibility (in the form of desire, for example), more tuned in to the fixity of power relations (in the form of capitalism), and less likely to buy the broken ideologies of uniqueness, American dreams, inclusivity, and respectability. The gaga generation, made up of men, women, and everyone else, knows that the future is now, greed (think Hummers) is crass, mutation is possible, and insurrection is here, and it is you, and we are already singing the crazy songs of a future world. And when you decide you are ready to go well and truly gaga, to leave behind the seeming rationality of contemporary life and love, when you are prepared to see through the lies of romance, the coercion of love and marriage, the fiction of equality and unity, when you are open to a new feminism, a gaga feminism that joins forces with the oppositional movements sweeping the globe, you will finally realize that we are already living in the future that we have always tried to imagine, a time and a place where the many say no to the few, the queer counsel the straight, the children teach their parents, and the lunatics, as the saying goes, have taken over the asylum. As the streets fill with the sounds of protest, the banks lose traction, the law loses credibility, the norm falters and collapses under the weight of its own contradictions, at that moment, you will be ready to say that we have all gone well and truly gaga, that we are staying gaga, and that the end of the old rings in a new set of possibilities out of which, hopefully, a few paths will lead us not home but into the playing field of a future that we cannot yet see, that we refuse to predict, and that will frame a new set of dreams. Lady Gaga may be the name now for a site of global popularity and global investments in difference, but this name too will change and what is gaga today will be something else entirely tomorrow. Let gaga feminism begin!

ACKNOWLEDGMENTS

This book was written in something of a frenzy in 2011 as new forms of protest took hold in cities around the nation and the world to protest the growing gap between a finance class and everyone else. The arithmetic of this difference, the famous 99 percent versus the 1 percent, certainly influences everything I've written about in this book, even though I began it before the protests took hold and ended it as they were on the verge of becoming a part of a new political reality. I want to acknowledge the occupation movements here as an inspiration and a source of hope.

I also want to thank Amy Scholder for helping me to conceive of this book, Gayatri Patnaik for allowing me to realize its final form, and Michael Bronski for patient, smart, and careful editing suggestions. Thanks to everyone at Beacon Press, especially Rachael Marks.

The image used on the cover came from the *Gaga Stigmata* blog, a wonderful place for hip and edgy writing on Lady Gaga, queer femininities, and popular culture. I would like to thank the artist, Angela Simione, and the cover designer, the brilliant and talented Nicole Hayward.

I hope this book will not embarrass the children in my life once they are old enough to read it—Renato and Ixchel, especially, but also my nephews and nieces and the many children I now know who are growing up in queer contexts. And I dedicate the book to my partner, Macarena Gomez-Barris, my favorite gaga feminist, my muse, y mi amor.

NOTES

Introduction: Going Gaga

1. Sheila Marikar, "Lady Gaga as Jo Calderone: Brilliant or Creepy?" ABCNews.com, August 29, 2011, http://abcnews.go.com/.

2. Perez Hilton, "Lady GaGa Opens Up 2011 VMAs as Jo Calderone!!" August 28, 2011, http://perezhilton.com/.

One: Gaga Feminism for Beginners

1. Susan Faludi, "American Electra: Feminism's Ritual Matricide," *Harper's Magazine*, October 2010, 29.

2. Ibid., 41.

3. Ibid., 40.

4. Camille Paglia, "Lady Gaga and the Death of Sex," *Sunday Times Magazine* (London), September 12, 2010.

5. Gayle Rubin, "The Traffic in Women: Notes on the 'Political Economy' of Sex," in *The Second Wave: A Reader in Feminist Theory*, ed. Linda Nicholson (London: Routledge, 1997), 27–62.

6. Ibid., 41.

7. Ibid., 42.

8. Judith Levine, *Harmful to Minors: The Perils of Protecting Children from Sex* (Minneapolis: University of Minnesota Press, 2002).

9. Ibid, 62.

10. Peggy Orenstein, *Cinderella Ate My Daughter: Dispatches from the Front Lines of the New Girlie-Girl Culture* (New York: HarperCollins, 2011).

11. Mary Spicuzza, "Slacker Guys and Striver Girls," *SF Weekly*, November 15, 2007.

12. David Kaufman, "Black Voters Are Pragmatic about Gay Marriage," *The Root*, March 4, 2011, www.theroot.com/.

13. Roderick A. Ferguson, *Aberrations in Black: Toward a Queer of Culture Critique* (Minneapolis: University of Minnesota Press, 2004).

14. Mignon Moore, *Invisible Families: Gay Identities, Relationships, and Motherhood among Black Women* (Berkeley: University of California Press, 2011).

Two: Gaga Genders

1. Shulamith Firestone, *The Dialectic of Sex: The Case for Feminist Revolution* (New York: Morrow, 1970), 10–11.

2. Sam Roberts, "51% of Women Now Living without Spouse," *New York Times*, January 16, 2007.

3. Naomi Klein, *The Shock Doctrine: The Rise of Disaster Capitalism* (New York: Metropolitan Books, 2007), 525.

4. Susan Faludi. *The Terror Dream: Fear and Fantasy in Post-9/11 America* (New York: Metropolitan Books, 2007).

5. Hanna Rosin, "The End of Men," *Atlantic*, July/August 2010, http://www.theatlantic.com/magazine/archive/2010/07/the-end-of-men/8135/2/.

6. Pamela Paul, "Are Fathers Necessary?" *Atlantic*, July/August 2010, http://www.theatlantic.com/.

7. Don Lattin, "Gay Monogamous Couple Are Brains behind Polygamy Show," *San Francisco Chronicle*, June 10, 2007.

8. Arlie Hochschild, with Anne Machung, *The Second Shift: Working Parents and the Revolution at Home* (New York: Viking, 1989).

9. Ibid., 4.

10. Avital Ronell, *The Telephone Book: Technology, Schizophrenia, Electric Speech* (Lincoln: University of Nebraska Press, 1991).

Three: Gaga Sexualities: The End of Normal

1. Mary Fischer, "Why Women Are Leaving Men for Lesbian Relationships," *O, The Oprah Magazine,* April 2009.

2. I write about these films extensively in my book *The Queer Art of Failure* (Durham, NC: Duke University Press, 2011).

3. Lori Gottlieb, *Marry Him: The Case for Settling for Mr. Good Enough* (New York: Dutton, 2010).

4. Lauren Berlant, *The Female Complaint: The Unfinished Business of Sentimentality in American Culture* (Durham, NC: Duke University Press, 2008), 13.

5. Daniel Bergner, "What Do Women Want?" *New York Times Magazine,* January 22, 2009.

6. Jenny Nordberg, "Afghan Boys Are Prized, So Girls Live the Part," *New York Times,* September 20, 2010.

7. Dan Bilefsky, "Sworn to Virginity and Living as Men in Albania," *New York Times,* June 23, 2008.

8. Saskia Wieringa, "Silence, Sin, and the System: Women's Same Sex Practices in Japan," in *Women's Sexualities and Masculinities in a Globalizing Asia,* eds. Saskia E. Wieringa, Evelyn Blackwood, and Abha Bhaiya (Basingstoke, UK: Palgrave Macmillan, 2009), 24.

9. Lisa Diamond, *Sexuality Fluidity: Understanding Women's Love and Desire* (Cambridge, MA: Harvard University Press, 2008), 3.

10. Dian Hanson, ed., *The Big Penis Book* (Cologne, Germany: Taschen, 2008).

11. Susan Faludi, *Stiffed: The Betrayal of the Modern Man* (New York: William Morrow, 1999).

12. Penelope Green, "Furniture Takes a Manly Turn," *New York Times,* September 15, 2010.

13. Ibid.

Four: Gaga Relations: The End of Marriage

1. "Is Gay Marriage Racist? A Conversation with Marlon M. Bailey, Priya Kandaswamy, and Mattie Udora Richardson," in *That's Revolting! Queer Strategies for Resisting Assimilation,* ed. Mattilda Bernstein Sycamore (Brooklyn, NY: Soft Skull Press, 2008), 89.

2. Nancy Polikoff, *Beyond (Straight and Gay) Marriage: Valuing All Families Under the Law* (Boston: Beacon Press, 2008), 147.

3. Ibid., 151.

4. Simone De Beauvoir, *The Second Sex*, trans. Constance Borde and Sheila Malovany-Chevallier, introduced by Judith Thurman (orig. 1949; New York: Knopf, 2009), 63.

5. Laura Kipnis, *Against Love: A Polemic* (New York: Pantheon Books, 2003).

6. Mary Elizabeth Williams, "Bridesmaids: A Triumph for Vomit, and Feminism." Salon.com, May 10, 2011.

7. A. O. Scott, "The Funnywoman, Alive and Well," *New York Times,* May 28, 2011.

8. Michelle Dean, "Bridesmaids: Am I Doing Being a Woman Wrong?" *The Awl*, May 16, 2011, http://www.theawl.com/.

9. Dean Spade and Craig Willse, "Freedom in a Regulatory State? Lawrence, Marriage and Biopolitics," *Widener Law Review* (2005): 311.

10. Fred Moten, "Gestural Critique of Judgment," in *The Power and Politics of the Aesthetic in American Culture,* eds. Ulla Haselstein and Klaus Benesch (Munich: Bacarian American Academy, 2007). Dayan's question was posed in *The Story of Cruel and Unusual* (Cambridge, MA: MIT Press, 2007).

11. Moten, "Gestural Critique of Judgment."

Five: Gaga Manifesto

1. James C. Scott, *Weapons of the Weak: Everyday Forms of Peasant Resistance* (New Haven, CT: Yale University Press, 1987).

2. Harsha Walia, "Letter to Occupy Together Movement," Rabble.ca, October 14, 2011, http://rabble.ca/.

3. The transcript of Zizek's remarks can be found at "Today Liberty Plaza Had a Visit from Slavoj Zizek," OccupyWallStreet, October 9, 2011, http://occupywallst.org/.

4. Slavoj Zizek, "Shoplifters of the World Unite," *London Review of Books,* August 19, 2011.

5. The Invisible Committee, *The Coming Insurrection* (Los Angeles: Semiotext(e), 2009).

6. Peter Kropotkin, *Mutual Aid: A Factor of Evolution* (New York: General Books, 2010).

7. Yoko Ono, *Grapefruit: A Book of Instructions and Drawings* (orig. 1964; New York: Simon and Schuster, 2000).

8. This quote circulates widely on the Internet. I found it here: "Lady Gaga: A Fashion Icon," http://www.millionlooks.com/.

9. Siddhartha Mukherjee, *The Emperor of All Maladies* (New York: Scribner, 2010), 452.

10. Del LaGrace Volcano, *Sublime Mutations* (Cape Town, South Africa: Janssen-Verlag, 2004).

11. Paolo Virno, *A Grammar of the Multitude: For an Analysis of Contemporary Forms of Life*, trans. Isobella Bertoletti, James Cascaito, and Andrea Casson (Los Angeles: Semiotext(e), 2003); Jacques Ranciere, *The Ignorant Schoolmaster: Five Lessons in Intellectual Emancipation*, transl. Kristin Ross (Palo Alto, CA: Stanford University Press, 1991).

12. "The Buys," *The Wire*, HBO, first aired June 16, 2002.